D0701420

TEACHING NONMAJORS

P. Sven Arvidson

TEACHING NONMAJORS

Advice for Liberal Arts Professors

State University of New York Press

Published by
STATE UNIVERSITY OF NEW YORK PRESS
ALBANY

© 2008 State University of New York

All rights reserved

Printed in the United States of America

No part of this book may be used or reproduced in any manner whatsoever
without written permission. No part of this book may be stored in a retrieval
system or transmitted in any form or by any means including electronic,
electrostatic, magnetic tape, mechanical, photocopying, recording, or otherwise
without the prior permission in writing of the publisher.

For information, contact
State University of New York Press, Albany, NY
www.sunypress.edu

Production and book design, Laurie Searl
Marketing, Michael Campochiaro

Library of Congress Cataloging-in-Publication Data

Arvidson, P. Sven.
    Teaching nonmajors : advice for liberal arts professors / P. Sven Arvidson.
        p. cm.
    Includes bibliographical references and index.
    ISBN 978-0-7914-7491-4 (hardcover : alk. paper)
    ISBN 978-0-7914-7492-1 (pbk. : alk. paper)
        1. Education, Humanistic. 2. College teaching—Handbooks, manuals,
etc. I. Title.

LC1011.A68 2008
378.1'2—dc22

                                                                    2007034481

                10   9   8   7   6   5   4   3   2   1

to Dr. Henry Rosemont Jr.,

teacher and friend

Contents

――――•◆•――――

Preface

————— ◆ —————

Perhaps I had visited the *Twilight Zone* of academia, but it was just an upper-level nursing class. The students dutifully took notes, arrived promptly and returned promptly from the break, and attended sharply to the intricate PowerPoint presentation and lecture. All of this could happen on a good day in one of my classes. What unsettled me was the students' appearance and demeanor. In a classroom of forty-five students, not one of them slouched in his or her seat for two hours. There were no torn or patched jeans. There were no caps or hooded sweatshirts pulled down to hide a face. No students sat alone. No pink hair, no green hair, no wild hair. All students had brought their course materials to class!

It took me awhile to come to grips with how this other world compares to my world. In that other world, the teachers are professional role models for students. The teacher is a nurse, the students are to be nurses. My students are not looking to be professors, much less philosophers. In that other world, all the teachers know all the students in the program, as in a big family. In a building built especially for their major, these students and professors see each other in the hallways, in classes, in gathering rooms, at regular functions over the span of four years. My students generally do not have the opportunity to take another course of mine—one term and out—and we are unlikely to have another conversation. In that other world, students have to pay attention to the course content because someone's life depends on getting it right. For my students, daydreaming in class is nonfatal. In that other world, students are trained early how to be competent and responsible students and as seniors, how to be professionals in a workplace. My students do not expect such training, nor would they accept it easily.

I primarily teach required "core" philosophy courses to students who are not philosophy majors. I enjoy having nursing majors and all the other majors one finds on a campus in my classes. Yet I envy the institutionalized

interconnectedness between these students and their departmental professors. My students are majors in business administration, accounting, social
work, engineering, history, religious studies, art, psychology, and so on. For
these students, my course is of secondary concern, and our relationship is
incidental to their future. I will not be their mentor. I will not be their advi-
sor. I will not be the professor who guides their senior project. But I will be
their teacher. This book specifically answers the question: What is good
advice for even better classroom teaching for liberal arts professors teaching
nonmajors in required courses? It answers this question using examples from
all of the major liberal arts and sciences disciplines.

The advice for better teaching to nonmajors naturally overlaps with the
advice for better teaching in professional preparation and upper-level major
courses. Good lecturing, effective assignments, successful class discussions,
and having sensible policies are similar no matter the audience and the professor's standing. However, the voice in this book is distinguished by consistent attention to the concerns of teaching nonmajors.

The first assumption throughout is that whether you are a part-time
adjunct instructor or a tenured professor, you are also probably a history professor teaching sociology majors, an English professor teaching electrical
engineering majors, an anthropology professor teaching philosophy majors, a
psychology professor teaching communications majors, a communication
professor teaching criminal justice majors, and so on. The second assumption
is that you are very busy. Hence this is a relatively short account of how to
make your classroom teaching even better. For some readers the advice will
be completely new, such as simple, innovative techniques to energize a class
by breaking up the lecture. For other readers the advice will be received more
like a reminder of what has been forgotten over the years. But for all readers
the advice is concise and easy to implement. The third assumption is that you
do not need hand-holding. What you want to do is engage these students
who are not majors in your discipline and are in your classroom because it is
required, not directly because they have chosen this course.

Can a teacher plan for greatness in the classroom? Yes. Can a teacher
guarantee it? No. Neither can this book. So as liberal arts professors primarily teaching nonmajors, our job is to consistently engage students with our
discipline. Since we cannot read their minds, we often descend into the mine
shaft without a headlamp. Perhaps the lamp temporarily flickers brightly as
we grade an assignment and get insight into how our students are thinking
and what they are thinking about. But in the classroom, day after day, we do
our best to set up the conditions for good teaching and learning, while maybe
feeling vulnerable, off balance, and at least slightly out of control.

What more can we do? We try to teach better, of course, determinedly.
We reflect and deliberate about how we are going to break up that day's lecture in a relevant way. We find the passion and wonder in that day's material
so that our lecture itself will inspire. We devise a provocative small-group dis-

cussion session that week in the course, so students get a chance to be social learners. We reimagine the usual assignment to make it into something challenging and creative. We constantly think about how to engage our students in that day's class, and we face up to problem students honestly, talking to them directly and wisely. We reflect deeply on our classroom policies and make sure not to slough off criticism that might be legitimate. And we care about improving or maintaining our performance on our institution's guidelines and criteria for excellent teaching, summarized numerically, also known as student ratings reports. This book attempts to answer concisely the question at the top of this paragraph: What more can we do?

Chapter 1 presents specific strategies for great lectures and discusses the key aspect of who you are in the classroom that makes lectures great. Chapter 2 gives immediately useful advice for breaking up lectures and maintaining student interest. It includes sections on discussions, props, artworks, and more. Chapter 3 describes how to use discussions to the best advantage of everyone involved. This chapter straightforwardly distinguishes types of discussion goals and structures. It also gives extended attention to the best use of student presentations (oral reports) in a course. Chapter 4 shows how to create wonderful, insightful assignments in any liberal arts discipline and specifically addresses innovative essay papers and exams, giving examples. This chapter also discusses grading and how to get students to read before class. Chapter 5 discusses policies for better classroom teaching, including surprising features of a good syllabus, the sense of an attendance policy, and various forms of communication with students. It also includes a special section on how to handle plagiarism cases. Chapter 6 treats student and professor problems or challenges, including teaching aggressively disinterested students and teaching special needs students. Chapter 7 discusses strategies for improving student ratings, freshly situating this improvement as the responsibility of the professor to the institution since the institution endorses this criterion of good teaching. Regardless of their controversial status, student ratings are widely held as firm evidence of good teaching by most administrators, so they are important in the careers of many professors. Chapter 8 concludes with a brief reflection on better classroom teaching.

I acknowledge a huge debt to my students over the years that I can never repay. Their sincerity, industry, laughter, dreams, and amazing intellectual curiosity have inspired me to try to be a better teacher and a better person. This book project has been a vague daydream for years, and many people have contributed to its reality in various ways, including all the professors, too many to name, who have indulged me when I want to talk about teaching, which is all the time. For our discussions on teaching, I am grateful to my fellow professors in the Peer Coaching of Teaching initiative at Seattle University's Center for Excellence in Teaching and Learning (CETL). Dr. Therese Huston, the founding director of CETL, and Dr. Paulette Kidder, associate dean of the College of Arts and Sciences at Seattle University, were instrumental in creating the conditions for this book. I thank the Seattle University philosophy department for its support and Kate Reynolds for her administrative assistance. I appreciate the comments by anonymous referees on how to improve the manuscript and thank Jane Bunker, Lisa Chesnel, and State University of New York Press for sharing my vision for this work. I also thank other professors from whom I have benefited greatly through conversations on teaching or from their superb example: Dr. Francis Ambrosio, Dr. Philip Barclift, Dr. John Bean, Dr. Jack Hettinger, Dr. Paul Kidder, Dr. Michael Klabunde, Dr. Timothy Lynch, Sr. Margaret McPeak, Dr. John Reuscher, and Dr. Ronald White. Dr. Henry Rosemont Jr., to whom this book is dedicated, has profoundly inspired my thoughts and feelings about what teaching can be and should be, and I am deeply grateful to him. Finally, and most important, I thank my wife, Julie, for her loving support in my life and work.

CHAPTER ONE

Give Better Lectures

Simply said, the more a lecture connects with students the better it is. The rub, of course, is the word *connect*. As discussed in the next chapter, songs, props, and personal experience are distinct ways in which anyone can increase the chances of connecting with students in the temporary suspension of straightforward lecture. But what about in the lecture itself? This chapter is not about the obvious things that can be picked up from any book on how to lecture: speak clearly, make eye contact, use the board, and so on. Instead it discusses the key aspect of who you are in the classroom and some specific strategies for better lectures in liberal arts and sciences courses for nonmajors.

DO WHAT YOU NATURALLY DO BEST—PASSION WINS

A methodical, earnest, low-key professor will appeal to some students, while a larger-than-life, boisterous professor will appeal to others. There are intense professors, aloof professors, shy professors, aggressive professors, each of whom can be an excellent lecturer. The first point is that no matter what you try to be, you will not please all of your students or even the majority. Therefore, extremes aside, it would be insane for the naturally boisterous professor to try to be low-key and the low-key professor to try to be boisterous in the classroom. The second point is that there is no one ideal lecture style. There is no one personality type that every lecturer should try to measure up to. What to do? Tell stories if you are a storyteller, use media if you are a tech junkie, carefully explain texts if you are a wordsmith, or orchestrate minishows if you are a director. Do what you naturally do best, for in giving better lectures what matters is not your personality type but your genuine passion. If you do not have passion and cannot find it, you lose, and students lose.

One famous scholar and teacher whose classes were always packed had a distinct, low-key style. He would stand behind the lectern and read carefully prepared statements for five to ten minutes. Then he would stand beside the lectern and try to expand on what he had already stated. Next he would go back to the lectern, and so on, repeating the process, over and over. Student attention was taut both while he stood behind the lectern and while he stood beside it. He never paced. He never ventured out into the aisles. He rarely used the board. In responding to questions, he simply stepped again beside the podium, answered the question, then stepped back behind it. How can someone like this—who mostly lectures from behind a podium or near it, is relatively low-key, uses little or no media—be the teaching star of a large, competitive department? His connection with the students was absolutely genuine. He did not try any tricks just to please them, he was incredibly well-prepared for the lecture, which included challenging himself to think about the legitimacy of his own interpretations of thinkers and texts, but most of all, he had genuine passion for the material, and it came across to the students academically and personally. His comportment was ceremonial and ritualistic, since this came naturally to him, and the students found this structure inspiring in the way that wedding ceremonies and swearing-in rituals can be inspirational. But all of this is empty without passion.

Whatever your personal style in the classroom, the underlying key to better lectures is maintaining passion about what you are doing. Students usually note this as "enthusiasm" in student ratings reports. This passion overrides the preference that the boisterous student has for the boisterous professor or the low-key student has for the low-key one. Yet this passion is not some inward, self-absorbed emotion or feeling that on occasion is successfully shared with students. The passion I am talking about is not selfish or disengaged from the audience, and it does not translate into bullying. The word *profess* is from the Latin *profiteri*—from *pro-*, before (the public), and *fateri*, to avow—so that as a professor *you avow or affirm your beliefs publicly*. Hence, passion, fervor, enthusiasm, love for your beliefs and knowledge are in your job description, and so is attention to your audience, the public. Being a professor in the classroom means you lecture passionately, publicly connecting with students. And if you live up to being passionate in this sense, it does not matter so much if you are shy or gregarious, intense or aloof, you will be a good lecturer. So among all the elements of your personality that will make for a good lecture on a specific day, passion wins.

DO THE UNEXPECTED

How do you start your classes? A former colleague of mine, Dr. Ronald White, teaching a course on human nature, would arrive in class one day as a robot. He did not dress any differently than usual, he simply arrived and announced that he would be filling in for the regular professor. Some students would laugh nervously; others yelled out that he *was* the regular professor! "Prove it," he said. So started an entertaining, mind-bending class session, even more so because it was totally unexpected. The lecture included the brief story of how the professor created him to stand in for the professor when he was not feeling well, or he wanted to do some other things during class time. The robot recharges in the basement of the professor's house, has all his same thoughts, and so on. He is absolutely the same as the professor. Of course, the lecture is a demonstration of the problems of artificial intelligence, what really makes a human being a human being, freedom, consciousness, and so on. And the professor lectures about all of this as the robot.

Not every class can be so dramatic. But doing, saying, or writing on the board the unexpected, especially at the beginning of a lecture class can re-energize the whole course and definitely makes that day's lecture unique. Some professors regularly start class by writing controversial statements on the board. For example, a literature professor focusing on the role of analogy in this discipline might write the following on the board to begin class, "Absolutely everything you know is known in comparison to something else." As lecture proceeds, and questions are asked, the class might arrive at some adjustments to this claim, which can be recorded on the board. These adjust-ments, along with the full-bore lecture information on analogy in literature and in life, are the pedagogical aims of this session. Yet the professor has started freshly, unexpectedly, memorably.

Every so often, in the middle of a required course for nonmajors, I feel the students are just going through the motions. I get the feeling that my pas-sion far outweighs theirs, and even some dedicated students give small signals (hardly stifled sighs, etc.) that indicate they resent the work I am assigning. Thankfully, this does not happen every term, but when it does I steel myself and do the following (which is also an example of breaking up lecture, as in the next chapter). I come into class and sit down in the chair up front, some-thing I never do in a large class. I ask, "You've read the assignment for today, what do you want to do with it?" The joker in the crowd responds he wants "to throw the book down three flights of stairs." The other joker shouts out that she wants "to get an A on the upcoming major assignment, just for read-ing the text." Still sitting, I take the responses somewhat seriously, asking them follow-up questions, trying not to disagree, trying not to say things such as, "Descartes is a classic in the history of ideas. You have to be nuts to dis-miss him so easily!" I nod my head and acknowledge their answers. Then I return to the question, "What do you want to do with this text?" Eventually the responses become more constructive: "I'd like to know where he is com-ing from. Why is he doing these meditations?" or "Why does he have to be so long-winded?" or "I don't get why this matters to me?" I invite other stu-dents to respond to each of these questions. Throughout the process there is a lot of silence, long, quiet moments of students looking at each other, look-ing at me, me looking at them, and me casually looking at my text, which they eventually do as well. The students become anxious. This may go on for a while until they have more or less decided to take responsibility for their learning and to enlist me to help them do that. Of course, this is simply a reiteration of the assumption on the first day of class: "I'm paying for a liberal arts college degree and as part of the agreement I will be exposed to work outside my major, and it's the professor's job to teach me this other information." Build in surprising moments in lecture courses, as part of the lecture, to reinvigorate a course, as in this example or to create a string of memorable nodes of intellectual excitement throughout the term.

KNOW YOUR STUFF

Some time ago I observed the class of a first-year teacher in philosophy. By all appearances, he (let us assume) knew the author he was teaching in great detail. The entire two-hour lecture (which unfortunately had only a comfort break as lecture relief, no discussion, props, etc.) was about one long philosophical argument and all of its subarguments. These were projected on a screen, and the professor proceeded from the beginning to the end, reading statement after statement, lecturing a moment or two on each assumption and conclusion. To the untrained eye, that is, the (glazed) student eye, this professor knew the subject matter in great detail. However, he did not, as became apparent in several misstatements of basic facts that nonmajor students would not know were false. This is important, but what also matters is that he did not know this text or this author well enough to genuinely connect with the students. He put together the long argument, which formed the whole of the material for the lecture session, from some exegetical source unknown to the students or from his graduate school notes, and proceeded to try to present it in an animated way. This argument projected on the screen was the curtain that separated him from the students, a curtain that kept him safe. As long as he followed this prefabricated script he would not be found wanting intellectually.

All of this is understandable for a first-year teacher, perhaps trying to teach and finish a dissertation at the same time. I remember using encyclopedias of philosophy and my graduate school notes as my lecture guides in my first year. However, this particular disconnect with students should be a one-time thing with respect to this particular material. I cannot imagine this professor teaching the same author, the same text, in the next term in the same way. It is his duty to know his stuff, to develop his own take on the author and the text, and to lecture better. The better lecture will come when he is freed from having to stand behind the curtain of formulaic ideas, ideas that are not his own. The better lecture will come from the confidence that a classroom leader, as lecturer, is able to show when he knows his stuff. In short, he will lecture well when he is able to more often pull the curtain back and say to his students, "This is what I think is important here . . ."

The veteran is also not excused from refreshing his or her knowledge. Listen carefully to student questions. Are they increasingly asking certain kinds of questions? Suppose over the last several years a sociology professor finds herself fielding more and more questions about the disabled or challenged populations and how we interact with them and the nature of social institutions with respect to this population, and so on. Suppose this professor is not that interested in this topic and has not researched it herself. She responds vaguely each time with something such as, "Well, there's been some sociological work on that, but not very much has been achieved yet." As in the case of the rookie, it is this professor's responsibility to know her stuff. She needs to start asking students about their interest in this topic when it comes up in class: "Interesting question. Are you studying about these populations in other classes?" She needs to ask other professors in other departments whether or not this is a hot topic in their field right now. (It probably is.) She needs to do enough research to be able to give at least a minimally better response: "Yes, many fields are investigating this right now. Let me write the titles of two books on the board for you to read to find out more."

Over the last several years, each time I teach a certain required core course at my institution, an upper-level philosophical ethics course for non-majors, more and more of my students have asked specific questions about the political philosophy of the classic and modern authors they read. In the past, I handled the questions as best I could and moved on. But the authors are a closed set—Aristotle, Kant, and Mill. They are included in any philosophical ethics course across the United States. This means with a one-time investment of targeted research, I could refresh myself on this topic enough to perennially connect better with what students are learning in their other courses (business, management, cultural studies, economics, literature, history), disciplines that have more recently featured political philosophy. Therefore, it is incumbent upon me not just to answer their questions as best I can but also to learn some political philosophy and rework lectures to draw out connections between ethics and politics and between courses for students. This connecting is a connecting to students that makes for better lectures.

CARE FOR QUESTION AND ANSWER

In our rush to get through our lecture material, we sometimes miss the significance of that moment when a hand goes up, and a student is ready to publicly enter into a discussion with the professor. We also often fumble the invitation for students to ask questions in the midst of a lecture.

Suppose a student raises his or her hand just as you are about to announce the amazing conclusion you have been building to for fifteen minutes. You have momentum, you have the class connected with you, but now everyone notices this hand. This is not an "interrupter" student (described in chapter 6). This is a good, well-meaning student who simply has a question at what for you is the wrong time. What do you do? You are not obligated to answer every question as it comes along, and given this scenario, interrupting your crescendo works against good pedagogy. Let us say you stop and invite the student to ask the question. Suppose it turns out that the next thing you were about to say was going to answer this question anyway, or that the student asks something totally offtrack. Now it is too late. The wind is gone from the sails, and you will have to tack to regain momentum. The first point is that as a lecturer you are under no obligation to immediately answer a student's question.

Let us say you waive off this student's question. Exactly what gesture do you use? All eyes are on you. Do you look at the student while you gesture or do you make the gesture in the student's general direction, in your peripheral vision? Do you hold up your hand to the student, with a "number one" index finger extended, and whisper "just a minute"? Do you make this gesture while looking exasperated at the interruption? Of course, all of this matters for classroom atmosphere for student questions. That is, each question matters in this way. Others will judge whether or not to participate and use this occasion as evidence. Your tone and demeanor are important in responding to a student question. Students rightly hate dismissive professors, professors who talk down to them from the supposed heights when they ask what they think is a decent question, so we should firmly but kindly ask a student to wait, when appropriate, rather than being dismissive. The second point, then, is to take care in how you ask a student to wait. Make eye contact, be firm, be kind, and do not make a big public deal out of it.

Sometimes you invite questions. Inviting questions as a way of breaking up lecture could have been discussed in chapter 2, but it is more pertinent here. At some point, every lecturer has asked, "Does anyone have any questions?" There are better ways to invite students to participate, but there is nothing wrong in itself with this phrase, any more than the standard retail phrase, "Can I help you?" The customer in the retail store knows the game and gives the standard response ("Just looking"). What matters in these cases of invitation is what happens next. Just as the retail salesperson should follow up with another kind of invitation ("Great, a new shipment of spectacular widgets has just arrived. Let me show them to you"), so should the professor. In the classroom, this invitation could include the very powerful tool of loud silence.

The experienced professor and salesperson know to silently wait in the midst of the invitation ritual and not try to fill the space just because the silence is slightly uncomfortable. A former colleague once invited me in to her (let us assume) class to observe the level of student participation. She said, "The problem is that students are very passive. They are not asking questions or making points in class, even when I invite them to." After about fifteen minutes of lecture, she asked, "Does anyone have any questions?" Two seconds later (not an exaggeration), she said, "Well then, let's continue."

Unlike the case where the lecturer is hoping that no one really has questions, this lecturer genuinely wanted them. The silence was too uncomfortable for her. Wait, look around, wait some more. Then rephrase the question, "What more can I tell you about this topic? What am I leaving out for you?" There may not be any questions, but you have made a solid invitation. If you truly want to have questions from students, if you want them to ask for clarifications, or to bring up problems, you need to ask carefully, and you will get them. And a major part of this care is learning to live with silence.

A big mistake professors can make in the lecture situation is to not answer the question asked and to take too long to do it. In certain lecture atmospheres, created by the professor, many students will not accept an invitation to ask a question for fear of becoming the "target" of the professor's lecture for the next fifteen minutes. I am not advising that you be curt, but try to be concise in responses. This concision will also greatly relieve pressure on getting all the course content accomplished for that day. Solving the problem of actually answering the question asked can require some brief preliminary questioning of the student by the professor to make the question more precise. This is time well spent. Without this, your five-minute answer, valuable time in many course formats, could be completely offtrack of the student's needs. For example, the student asks, "I don't understand how Marx's political theory is supposed to lead to a utopia. What am I missing?" The professor responds, "What exactly do you disagree with? Is it the determinism in his theory, the idea of a utopia, or something else?" The student continues, "I don't disagree. I just don't see how alienation is connected with utopia." Now the request has become more specific, and a relevant answer can be made.

AVOID LECTURE TRAPS

There are many more lecture traps than the four I discuss below. I choose these four because they are both common and seductive. In the same way an animal falls into a trap, pursuing some lure that proves satisfying, these lecture traps each come with powerful lures that keep the professor in a loop of mediocre teaching or wasteful time management.

FILL-IN-THE-BLANK TRAP

A common lecture trap, the "fill-in-the-blank" lecture style goes something like this. The professor asks, "Napoleon was imprisoned because . . . ?" and some student fills in the blank. "Right," says the professor. "And they imprisoned him on this island rather than put him to death. What was the name of the island, and where was it?" Students respond; the professor continues. "This led Napoleon's friends to do . . . what?" And so it goes on and on. Sitting through a class session of fill-in-the-blank lecturing is exhausting. The stops and starts make the presentation fragmentary rather than cohesive, and the fill-in-the-blank approach to "classroom participation" is more appropriate to some level of precollege education, perhaps even middle school. The professor will argue that there is class participation throughout the session, but there is no full flowering of participation, just very formal and controlled sprouting followed by constant pruning.

RUBE GOLDBERG TRAP

Another trap is to use elaborate means to explain something very simple. But if you have spent a lot of time preparing an exercise or piece of media or working out this cluster of related concepts, it is very difficult to move it to the back of your preparation folder for the course. For example, in a section of a course dedicated to critical thinking, I spent some time preparing an elaborate exercise to explain a relatively simple and minor point about logic. I kept subjecting classes to this exercise because I thought it was brilliant. It took half of a class session to explain to the students what to do and how to do it and to lecture about it. Behind the scenes I spent way too much time fine-tuning this exercise. How could I give it up with so much invested, and since the students seemed to enjoy it? Keeping an exercise like this is seductive, but it is also like building a Rube Goldberg machine. (This is the annual engineering contest where some mundane task is accomplished using many more steps than necessary, just like making a major deal out of a minor point.) Therefore, as a professor, keep in mind return on investment as you start spending inordinate amounts of time on a boutique type of preparation for lecture.

COVERING ALL THE MATERIAL TRAP

It is better to deeply introduce your students to less material than superficially introduce them to more material. You do not have to cover it all. Do not allow yourself to be oppressed by the full weight of the material or by the need for completeness of the material to be covered. Your students are not being prepared for some proficiency exam in your discipline, unlike a civil engineering student who may have to pass a test. Yes, you must impress your students with the material but not by the fact that there is a lot of it. They know that the field is large, and if they already think that the discipline is marginally important in their lives, then adding more quantity just increases the sense of marginality. When you try to cram in too much material, there is no space for silences, for question-and-answer periods, for dyad and triad discussion groups, for breaking up lecture.

DISTANCING TRAP

Another lecture trap is teaching from a distance. Teaching from a distance is when you can get through a lecture (or a course) impersonally, safely. There is no risk, no "professing." A codependent relationship forms between professor and students such that the students enable the professor to be a mediocre lecturer. Once this pattern is established students will allow you to teach from a distance, to teach disinterestedly. Early in a course, they will naturally resist detached, disinterested teaching. The students take the initiative, before routine is established, to show you that they do not want to be bored in class. Various students will ask questions in class; various students will approach you after or before class. Yet as the term proceeds, the students will allow a comfortable routine to develop in which they silently consent to be less engaged, while you silently consent to teach impersonally. They are students at a distance, and you are a teacher at a distance. Everyone is more or less waiting out the end of the term.

For example, I once taught a large, required, upper-division course for nonmajors in which 10 percent of the students happened to be autistic (see also chapter 6). This was my first real experience with autism in the classroom. The course ended up being a mediocre experience for almost all the students and for myself, because they answered "yes" to my quiet request to let me teach safely, at a distance. Since I had taught this particular course a lot (once I taught it six times in an academic year) I always tried every trick I could to keep it fresh for myself. I changed books, read new background material, tried new assignments, and generally self-motivated to give the students a first-rate experience. But this term I took the easy way out. It was the end of a seemingly endless academic year, I was bored and distracted, and I was confused about how to be both naturally inspired for nonautistic students and clearly procedural for my autistic students, who were recording the course lectures. I chose to squelch sparkle in the classroom for the dullness of being thorough. This choice was not my only option, and it was not even clear to me at the time that this was the choice I had made. The students eventually followed my lead. I taught at a distance. Instead of engagement between us, I let them go, and they let me go. Ever since, when I feel the distance increasing between me and my students, and me and my material, I become very uneasy and deeply question how I am going to shake the feeling of comfort and safety of business as usual and resume professing.

EXPLOIT ANALOGIES AND DIAGRAMS

St. Thomas Aquinas famously claimed that human thinking is primarily analogical. It is somewhat difficult to produce analogies, yet no one thing sparks the imagination of an audience better than a well-struck analogy. All of the disciplines in the liberal arts and sciences work with difficult, sometimes abstruse concepts. It is your job to find analogues to use in your lecture. Analogies used in lecture can uniquely crystallize a complicated concept and lead to insightful questions about that concept's rightness or wrongness. There are several standard or general structures for analogical representation that can be great places to start. Many are well worn, such as the mechanical analogy (a deterministic process, step-by-step, build-up and release of pressure, etc.). But within such a general analogy others unfold, perhaps equally well worn, such as a cog in the wheel or a computer hard drive. There are nature analogies (flowerings, nurturing, cyclings, icebergs, geological strata), animal analogies (packs, nestings, stalkings), biological, chemical, musical, historical, theatrical, linguistic, literary, and so on. Choose your analogy with your audience in mind. For example, to target economics majors in your classroom use a business analogy, to target nursing majors use a medical analogy. As a lecturer, one of your most important jobs is to find good illustrative parallels that light up a clearing in the mind of the student. Analogies are the bullet-train to this station.

Diagrams can also be very powerful. Most professors in the liberal arts have occasion to draw a diagram on the board. It could represent a hierarchy, a cluster, a correspondence, cause and effect, a network, a Venn diagram, and so on. For example, a professor wants to draw a cause-and-effect relationship between two things. The professor asks, "How does the mind influence the world?" On one side goes a circle with eyes (the mind), and across from it the word *world*, with an arrow in between. He or she reverses the arrow for the world influencing the mind or makes a double arrow. One can imagine that versions of this rudimentary causal diagram are used in sociology class (institutions affecting groups), in psychology (mother on son), in communication arts (media on consumer), in history (war on peasant), and so on, with the arrow direction switched when needed. A professor may leave this diagram up for the whole session and refer back to it often. It will certainly be recorded into the student notebooks. The trick is to push yourself beyond this kind of standard diagram so that the complex relationships between concepts in a theory, or in a book, can be linked in visual ways for the student. For example, straight lecturing in a political science class on the concept of 'welfare' and its related themes is very different than slowly building a diagram on the board of the relationship between the welfare concept and themes as the lecture unfolds. It takes intense, creative reflection and more preparation than usual, but the payoff is huge. Where to start? Is the concept of welfare more like a circle in a circle, or is it more like a network of relationships? Is it both, or neither? Is it part of a hierarchy, a hierarchy and cause and effect, and so on? Even if the diagram is half-baked, this is fine. Students will be happy to help you clean it up, modify it, and add to it, if invited.

GIVE STUDENTS THE NOTES

Almost every professor has personal lecture notes, and it is appropriate that some of these notes remain in the professor's sole possession. But many professors in lecture classes work off of notes in the classroom and expect students to transcribe these aural sayings into good notes comparable to the original. Why not arrange to give most of the originals instead? Moreover, in many lecture classes, how well the student knows the professor's notes becomes a main criterion for assessment, for example, as in-class exams. Predictably, these student notes are often pale imitations of the professor's notes. If it is very important for the students to correctly write down definitions, processes, conceptual relations, and so on, then the professor can guarantee that there are fewer misunderstandings by putting these notes together for the student.

One way to accomplish the notes giveaway is to devise a *course notebook*. (For skills-oriented classes, it can be more of a *course workbook*.) Students bring this soft-bound book to class just like any other textbook needed that day. It could contain a syllabus, including course schedule, policies, justifications for the policies (if needed), printed out in-class displays such as overhead transparencies, PowerPoint, typical formulations for a day's class that the professor expects to write on the board, assignments, and so on.

With respect to better lectures, there are advantages and pitfalls for students and for professors in giving students the notes. The advantages for students can be remarkable. First, there is less frantic note taking, and more genuine listening, including eye contact between the professor and the student. Second, depending on the medium chosen, for example a course notebook, students have a ready-made, very handy "notebook" on which to take additional, more specific notes. Third, students already have the notes and can be encouraged to look at them as they prepare for class that day; consequently, student discussion is more advanced, and student questions are better. If the notes are not the kind that students can read and understand ahead of time (because they are too schematic), there is still better opportunity for more advanced discussion in class since students are not writing large swaths of notes. Fourth, important points are sure to be in students' hands in exactly the manner the professor wants them to be. Definitions, explanations of processes or cycles, statistics, and exegeses of difficult texts are all formulated exactly as they should be, which means that the student can have confidence in the information.

Giving away a larger number of appropriate notes also holds distinct advantages for you, the professor. In addition to the obvious benefit of better learning on the part of students, creating a course notebook or otherwise organizing and making available in class most of the notes results in more efficient course management. First, your own files become more organized. Second, updating or refining course content is much easier. For example, a course notebook is prepared once and simply modified thereafter for each additional time the course is taught. This saves time, minimizes errors of omission in course content, and allows a higher-level starting point for daily lectures and course improvement. Third, the course appears more organized to students. This is obviously an advantage to students, but it is also an advantage to you. The perception and one would suppose the reality of a better organized course translates into more student independence since there is less remedial explanation about what is happening in the course and when. This frees time for the professor. Fourth, but not directly related to improving lectures, in a course notebook the professor can include special elaborations on policy without weighing down the syllabus (see chapter 5). These might include general directions and expectations for term papers, justification for attendance policies, and examples of what counts as plagiarism. You could also include special additional information about resources such as writing or counseling centers, supplemental texts, biographies, history time lines, and pertinent quotes.

There may also be some disadvantages to giving away the notes. First, students can feel overwhelmed with too much information. Reading and learning the additional notes becomes an extra course requirement in some students' minds, in addition to other course textbooks, course Web pages, guest speakers, tests, and so on. Second, when I once took it upon myself to create a paragraph-by-paragraph exegesis of an extremely difficult text, a fair number of students reported in student ratings comments that having this in the course notebook constrained their own creative thinking. I had interceded in their authentic engagement with the text. They were right. I subsequently moved the exegesis to a Web site and made reading my commentary truly optional. Third, if a course requires attendance, an incredibly detailed course notebook can appear to work against the need for students to be physically in class on a particular day. When thinking through these three challenges in your own course, the overarching strategy is to keep the notes simple and relevant. Only include what is essential or truly helpful.

Three more challenges are worth mentioning. Some courses or some large modules of courses are best arranged in a way where the information is revealed slowly, composed out of simpler building blocks until the full picture is exposed. Students who see the more complex information by looking ahead in a course notebook may be disheartened or confused. Thus, the course notebook idea may not work for all courses or all parts of a course, depending on learning objectives. Also, once the notebook is published for the students, it enters the public realm. This may be a concern if the information is controversial, inaccurate or unscholarly, or it can be misconstrued, for example, because it is taken out of context. Finally, giving students the notes frees up time for breaking up lecture or using discussions, but it also streamlines timing. I have been caught off guard more than once by the efficiency of giving students the notes—for example, a half-hour left in a session with nothing planned. The other side of the coin is that once I got used to having more free time in a lecture period, I was able to break up lecture more often and facilitate more creative discussions (chapters 2 and 3).

THE CHALLENGE OF POWERPOINT

When I assign students to give a formal oral presentation to the rest of the class, I include the requirement that they use *one* form of media in their presentation. A typical list is the following: "blackboard use, a prop, audio/visual equipment (videotape, stereo, projecting computer), overhead transparency, poster, or other media." Overwhelmingly, when my students read this list they assume that I mean they must use this one piece of media *in addition to* PowerPoint! It is not news to anyone in academia or business that PowerPoint is ubiquitous: many students expect professors to use it, and many professors use it regularly. It is also not news that PowerPoint is controversial and loathed by some users and nonusers alike. In this section, I will not tangle with the well-known advantages and disadvantages of PowerPoint or give generic advice widely available, such as, do not put too much information on each slide, and be consistent in styling and animation of slides. Instead, I will focus on one of the most interesting challenges that professors face in using PowerPoint in lecturing to nonmajors in the classroom: PowerPoint commands a student's attention in an almost automatic way. It immediately becomes what one should focus on in the room. PowerPoint is vivid, huge, and alternately engaging or boring (just like TV). As professors how do we keep it engaging?

First, break away from PowerPoint periodically. When your students seem to be disengaged, and even to your own ears you are "droning on," what do you do? Many of us just keep droning on, even though we know better, perhaps increasing our volume. But it just takes a moment to refresh the room. Blank the screen as a signal that for the moment the focus is no longer on the PowerPoint screen (for example, on a keyboard press the B key). Ask for questions, let there be some silence, ask how they are doing, or otherwise break up the presentation in the same way a lecture might be refreshed (see chapter 2). When you are ready, ask them if they are ready and then resume the presentation. It is amazing how effective these little breaks can be. Also, you can build such breaks into your presentation ahead of time, perhaps with a slide that gives a lovely, natural scene—an amazing waterfall or a sweeping desert. (Who says such a slide has to be on topic?) This is your classroom, it should have your style, at least subtly. In your students' eyes, everything from what you wear to how you speak is already an expression of your unique style, so slip in a fun slide at the appropriate spot. Breaking up the presentation and reengaging students in this way shows your "human side" as a lecturer and makes sense.

Second, determine the best mechanics for notetaking when you use PowerPoint. There are lots of choices. At one extreme, a professor can give students hard copies of *all* slides and presenter notes. This is expensive and perhaps wasteful; it can also increase student passivity. At the other extreme, students must take notes while witnessing the PowerPoint presentation itself with no handouts or follow-up material and no posting of the presentation online for students to review. A better approach is for professors to provide modified notes later, for example online, perhaps incorporating student in-class questioning and response and giving attribution to students by using their names. Students then have their own in-class notes (and are somewhat

active in class) and the professor's notes. Another common strategy is to
economize by printing out six of the slides on one sheet of paper, on which
students can take notes. Often the print in this format and the space in
which to take quality notes are both too small. One solution is to manipu-
late the handout by using Microsoft PowerPoint and Word together. In PowerPoint, choose File and Send To and Word to custom arrange the information for students in Microsoft Word with slides or without, with notes or
without. In any case, clearly tell students when and what to write if it really
matters, just as in lectures. Also, give better pacing for note takers by revealing bullets on a slide one at a time, rather than all at once. Finally, if a professor encourages or allows students to bring their laptop computers to class,
then the students can take their own notes in the "Click to Add Notes" section below each slide. This is incredibly efficient and seems like a perfect
solution if all students have access to laptops. However, there are at least two
reasons for concern here. One, many students will secretly use social net-
works (Facebook, MySpace) when given the chance. (I have witnessed this
countless times as a back-of-the-room classroom observer.) Two, students are
now primarily engaged with their own private screens, not with the public
screen up front and with the rest of the class. Since disengagement is exactly
the chief problem in teaching nonmajors, I do not allow laptop use while
class is in session, unless it is by arrangement for learning disabled students.
It severely decreases eye contact, tends to decrease attention to what the
professor and fellow students are saying, tends to increase hiding behaviors
(such as students not being a part of class by hiding behind big laptop
screens), and gives students too much temptation to surf the Web rather
than be involved with class. Of course, each professor must weigh the pros
and cons of such a policy for themselves.

Third, know your room lights, and use them well. This sounds like
straightforward advice, but one of the first things many occasional Power-
Point presenters do is turn *off* the lights. When the lights go down past a
certain point, the students disengage. A room does not have to be dark for
effective PowerPoint viewing. Find the balance by sitting in your own students' chairs early in the term with the PowerPoint on. A room too dark
encourages all sorts of hiding behaviors, including napping. It discourages
good note taking, especially for some students whose eyes may be weaker in
uncertain light. In a darkened room, the possibility for discussion is
decreased, cues are hardly seen, and eye contact is more difficult. As with
the first-year professor discussed above, it is easy for a professor to "hide
behind" the PowerPoint presentation. In a dark room, the professor's ges-
ticulations, facial expressions, eye contact, and other possibly engaging
behaviors are lost.

PowerPoint can be a wonderful medium in liberal arts courses since it
can present textual information vividly, and it can dramatically show pho-
tographs, artwork, or videos and even show dynamic processes through clever

slide arrangement. But like any of our vehicles of teaching, it should be used judiciously, along with lecture, discussion, and the various methods of breaking up lecture discussed in chapter 2.

BRIEFLY DEBRIEF YOURSELF

Your lecturing is bound to be better if you have more time to prepare, and you have some historical sense of how that particular lecture has fared in the past. At the end of a day of teaching, or in preparation for the next class, you should briefly write what you did in the latest class session. This log or journal process has been described by a number of authors. Although some call it a "teaching diary" this could mean a lot of things. For example, the teacher could record anything he or she is feeling in connection with that day's class: "I was feeling nervous at first about the student presentations, because I knew some weren't very prepared, and also because I was a little late to class today." The kind of journal or chronicle I would like to focus on is simply a log of major events in the classroom on that day: materials used for preparation, the sequence of presentation in the classroom, general student response. For example, did you show the film clip after or before the discussion on Central America? Did the students still discuss the film, even though it was shown after the Central America discussion? For many professors, it is unlikely they will remember these details a year later, and this means more preparation time or more anxiety about how to order that day's events the next time the course is taught. Also, next time you do not have to reinvent that session, hence less preparation. If you have sessions of two hours or longer, it is difficult and time consuming to arrange all the material into sensible events within the classroom. Keeping such a log of the series of events gives a wonderful high-level starting place for better lecturing the next time the course is taught.

When you debrief yourself each teaching day by making an entry in a log or chronicle of that day's events, you are also creating a record of which activities are worthwhile and should be kept and which should be changed or dropped. You record winners, problems, or fixes with regard to class lectures, examples, timing, or discussion instructions. Good history repeats itself, and bad does not. Next time you teach the course, if the same materials are used, starting points in preparation are much more developed. If the course has a different time frame, for example if it moves from a longer to a shorter class session, you can better estimate what can and what cannot be achieved in the new time frame. An easy way to record the information is to use the course schedule from the syllabus as a template for the log and simply add the appropriate entry under each date of class (I thank Dr. Paul Kidder for this template idea).

At the end of the course, based on student comments in assessments, you can append trends from the student's point of view to this particular course's journal and save it. It should be easy to see how powerful such a record can be the next time you prepare the course. Also, the feeling of the course and the crucial details of what went on in that course cannot adequately be reconstructed many months later. This teacher assessment of the student assessment of the course needs to be done soon after student ratings or evaluations are made available, and it has to be combined with written responses, which for most professors is easily done in a computer file stored in a folder with the course materials or appended at the end of the daily log.

CHAPTER TWO

Break Up Lectures

⸻ ◆ ⸻

It is rare for a professor to successfully fill the entire class period with straight lecture, whether it is an hour or three hours. A number of students seem programmed to become disengaged after about fifteen minutes of lecture. We have all seen the glazed eyeballs, the hardly stifled yawns, and aggressive passive-aggressive displays of disinterest, such as the student whose actions say "Well . . . do or say something important, and I will stop reading my accounting book right now." How does a professor provide relief—reenergizing the room around something worthwhile or pertinent? A former colleague of mine was famous for breaking up lecture by suddenly jumping up on the desk at the front of the class and lecturing from the heights to half-amused, half-terrified students. That certainly livened up his classroom, but what about the rest of us? Discussion, props, songs, in-class reading and writing, visual artwork, films, personal experience, and comfort breaks are successful and relevant ways to rejuvenate the classroom lecture.

USE RELEVANT CLASS DISCUSSION

Discussion is the most popular method professors use to break up the tedium of lecture, but there is an art to a good discussion exercise. Types of in-class discussion tasks can vary widely, so there are no hard and fast rules. But there are some general guidelines:

• Have a clear goal for the students and for the professor. These goals may not be the same goals.
• Think in terms of two, three, or four students; small groups generally work best since they decrease hiding behaviors and increase likelihood of equitable participation.

- Assign a scribe for the group; this crystallizes the task and formalizes the group.
- Attend to timing. Do you desire a short break-up task of two minutes or an elaborate multistage whole-period discussion? Debrief for almost as long as the discussion itself took to accomplish.

Since I talk about discussions in chapter 3, I will outline here the specific use of discussion for breaking up lecture.

Use a dyad discussion to quickly reenergize or redirect a class session. A dyad is created by simply asking students to "turn to one other student in the class and complete the following task." For example, on a day where course content concerns feminist material, students can be asked to discuss whether men and women really do think differently. Dyads are good for quick "break-ups" because it is merely one-on-one and dyads do not usually require physically rearranging chairs, backpacks, and other materials. Consider using this technique at least once a week, if not every class session. "Debriefing"—which is polling and questioning for discussion results—can be done very selectively and briefly, as a segue into the next facet of lecture. Most dyads used to relieve and advance lecture material should be kept under five minutes and probably do not need a scribe.

Use a triad or slightly larger group for longer discussions, at least ten minutes. These groups will need a more substantial task and should have a scribe assigned. One way to make a task more substantial is to create stages to the task. Using the above example and a larger group, the next stage of the feminist discussion might ask the students to list the kinds of evidence that would support their conclusion: anecdotal, biological, literary, historical, sociological, psychological, or religious, for example. In this example, the professor has in mind a general interdisciplinary point about methodology and what counts as evidence and knows that one of the aims of the ensuing lecture is to contextualize the methodology of the feminist approach the students have read in their text. Another way to move from one stage of discussion to the next is to have dyads become groups of four by rearranging themselves, and then arriving at results anew as a larger group, but this time with a scribe.

PROPS

Students love props. A prop is any hands-on artifact that helps the professor introduce or demonstrate some concept. One reason they work so well is because students often get to see a side of the professor that is not otherwise revealed. For example, where did this guy get that South American blow dart gun? They can be simple or elaborate. For instance, when I discuss the concept of "yin-yang" I often bring in a "smasher" disk from the old children's game Pogs which is emblazoned with the swirly, fishlike yin-yang symbol. Students want to play with it, they are interested in it, some reminisce, and it enables my point about East-West cross-fertilization, or about symbols. If I did not have the toy I could bring in a small Korean flag or a bumper sticker with the symbol. That same week of classes, to make a point about the crucial concept of 'emptiness' in the East and how it is relatively unimportant in the West, I have students pass around an ornate, small metal bowl in class and ask them to describe something about the bowl ("It has handles," "It is shiny metal," etc.). I stop the passing soon after one student gives the one response I am looking for ("The bowl is empty") and then proceed to discuss this kind of answer with them and continue lecture. In this case, I have previewed an important point I will discuss in lecture, and everyone gets a respite from a whole period of lecture.

The trick to using props is to recognize opportunities to use them and to actively think about how props fit into that day's lecture. For some types of courses or classes a prop is virtually required. For example, in a class session on birthing emergencies in a nursing course a professor is likely to use dolls to demonstrate the various points. In a psychology course section on the brain, a model of a brain is used. But in many liberal arts courses it is not so apparent when a prop can be used. It takes creativity to recognize opportunities. For example, an English professor discussing a period novel that students are reading can bring in some artifacts from the era. How is a feather boa around your neck for creating class interest? A simple moment can temporarily change the atmosphere of the room so that everyone can regroup. Upon returning from a trip to Athens, I started a new term and was teaching Aristotle. I decided to bring to class some Greek coins and bills I had left over. After about twenty minutes of lecture, I passed around the coins while I told them about Athens, old and new. The students were awestruck by this prop. I was pleased and very surprised by their reaction. There was no big philosophical point to be made on the tails of this prop, but it certainly galvanized the imagination in their heads for Aristotle's time and the Greek legacy.

In preparation for each class session, you have to ask what the reading discusses that can also be a prop. What can I bring in to break up the lecture? Does the reading use examples or illustrations that you might have around the house: billiard balls, orchids, a flashlight, a toaster? Students' props may also be used with their permission: a diamond ring, a cell phone, a lighter, a hat. How? Using props takes imagination: a diamond ring (in discussion of the ritual of marriage in an anthropology class), a cell phone (in discussion of voter access, to call the White House or the mayor in a political science class), a lighter (in discussion of early childhood learning—we do not touch a hot stove twice—in a human development class), a hat (to demonstrate hiding behaviors in a sociology class).

Finally, do not overlook the power of bringing in books, journals, or publishing house catalogs to pass around. For various levels of introductory classes, required courses taught mostly to nonmajors, it can be especially useful to pass around well-laid-out publishing house catalogs that you receive in the mail. For example, when I teach an introductory course in philosophy, one day I bring in the latest catalog from some big philosophy publishing house and pass it around, asking students to read at least two descriptions of advertised books. Students see that the field is larger than they thought ("I didn't know there was political philosophy"), and it serves to help introduce them to the field in a small way. In a more targeted way, bringing in other books by some great author being currently discussed in the course is a wonderful prop. Instruct the students to scan the table of contents or the index to get a feel for what is being discussed in this other work. Or if it is written in a different style (for example, a novel) have each student read to themselves several sentences on any page, when it is passed to them. This takes the student away from the current lecture for a minute so is a breaking up of the lecture experience, but the break is well worth the price. An issue of a scholarly journal can serve the same function.

SONGS

A great way to break up lectures is to use music. Play the songs themselves. We have all seen the professor in some department or other who is off to class with a big "boom box." It may look cliché, but songs can be very effective in widening the scope of the classroom experience and chasing off boredom (or at least for that day). And if you are lucky enough to snag a classroom with a built-in sound system, you do not need to lug the boom box. Of course, a laptop computer could substitute. Finding myself without a song I believed I needed in that particular lecture session, I had a student volunteer to download the song on her laptop computer during a class session and play it aloud when I was ready.

The use of a song in the class period is almost always a function of the lyrics. That is, the lyrics get across the message of the day, but in a poetic, aural format. So it is advisable to put the lyrics on the board or on overhead, so students can follow along when you play the song. This may just be a stanza or two or just the one line refrain that sums up your point. When I taught Nietzsche recently, it struck me that the contemporary heavy metal band Evanescence had recently produced an album whose lyrics captured well some of Nietzsche's points. I wrote the two stanzas of the most pertinent song on the board at the beginning of class. Later, when it was time to break up the lecture, I formally introduced the statement on the board and played the song. The song did double duty. It reexpressed Nietzsche's point in a contemporary way, and it gave relief to the lecture session. In another course, this time in the midst of a lecture about empathy, I simply wrote on the board the artist (Gladys Knight and the Pips) and the name of the song ("Midnight Train to Georgia") and the one line I took to illustrate the sense of empathy ("I'd rather be in his world, than be without him in mine"). I played the song and used this break in the lecture to then resume lecture now making specific points about empathy and private versus shared worlds. A former colleague teaching American history to nonmajors, would bring in his guitar and sing union songs!

Unlike most other ways to break up course lecturing, playing a song recording can make the professor feel odd. This is because no one is doing anything in the front of the room or elsewhere, no one is sure where to look (it is not primarily about visual display), and listening to music can be a more private experience for most people than watching a performance or lecture. The professor must resist the temptation to fill the space with anything more than the song while it is playing. If you feel like you are really experimenting by playing a song, if you feel out of your element and maybe even embarrassed to not be doing anything for three minutes, then good. For some departments and professors, playing a song in class is extraordinary. And this is exactly what a teacher wants to happen in the classroom for successful pedagogy. After class, students will volunteer other artists and songs that parallel your choice. Since this is what the students themselves are listening to, this information is valuable for the next time you use a song in class.

IN-CLASS READING AND WRITING

In-class reading and writing can be used as stand-alone strategies or as part of a combination to break up lectures. In-class reading and writing means that for several minutes, students are instructed to read to themselves or write in their notebook in response to a question or task. You can direct students to read to themselves a particular passage that the lecture is going to address. Often this is a passage they have already read in preparation for class. Why have them read it again? Three main reasons: it breaks up the lecture format, it freshens the crucial passage for the student, and it allows for discussion of larger passages as a whole that would be too much to read aloud for consequent commentary.

In-class writing is most often used as a prelude to in-class discussion. The student is able to sort out his or her own thoughts on the assigned subject before having to consider fellow students' ideas. Students reflect privately and write about the issue for a couple of minutes then enter into small group discussion ready to deepen their reflections. If discussions are not proceeding well in a particular course or tend to lack focus, this strategy of "prewriting" is worth trying. A variation is to have students pass their writing along, so others can add to it.

But in-class writing can also strongly stand alone. For example, within a lecture on the work of a contemporary playwright, the professor is about to discuss the concept of 'luck' in the plays. Instead, the professor asks students to reflect on examples of luck in the plays and to write a long, one-sentence description about the role of luck in the works. A short debriefing can ensue where the professor asks several students to read their sentences, although this is not necessary. The professor now proceeds to talk about the concept, and students are able to compare their own ideas to the professor's and (hopefully) ask questions. The whole process of divergence from lecture takes about five minutes and refreshes the classroom atmosphere. The writing may or may not be collected.

As a substitute for the standard "Does anyone have any questions?" used by nearly all professors, the students can be instructed to write their own questions. For instance, "Write one good question about this playwright that is not yet answered for you but that you think is important." After the several minutes it takes for the students to complete this assignment, the professor can poll some of the students and attempt to answer the questions or simply collect them to respond to later. Alternatively, the professor can ask that those students who would really like an answer but have not yet received one to email the question to the professor. Lecture has been suspended while students have reflected in class about the material and written something about it, and students with burning questions are given an avenue to follow up on their concerns (that few will choose to do so does not diminish the fact that lecture has been broken up and they have reflected about and written on the material).

Many professors require students to come prepared each week or even each class with a written statement of some kind, for example, an outline or a reflection on the reading (see chapter 4). This daily writing can be used as a platform for in-class reading or writing. Now and then, papers can be exchanged, and students can be directed to read another student's writing for that day. This in-class reading can then be followed by discussion or in-class writing. As a springboard to in-class writing, students can be instructed to add three more sentences to the paper they had just read and try to continue and deepen the other student's ideas. If students will be reading each other's "reflections," it is a good idea for them to be forewarned that the professor is not the only person to read their thoughts for that day.

VISUAL ARTWORK

Almost everything you will lecture about has a corresponding story in the visual arts of the times. One does not need to be an art historian to be able to make a connection for students between the material being taught and the corresponding Zeitgeist represented through artists' eyes. Displaying an artwork is a fantastic way to break up the lecture routine while enhancing course content.

The artwork can be displayed on any kind of projector or even on a computer screen. But the best way to use an occasional artwork is to print off a color copy. If you or your department do not have a color printer, most schools have a tech department that handles these requests. If all else fails, a neighborhood print/copy store will print it for a couple of dollars. In any case, the print can be held up while you introduce it and then passed around. Do not underestimate the role of tactile engagement in the classroom (see props above). It can also be taped to the classroom board for display.

Finding an example of the desired work of art is incredibly easy since the advent of online search engines. For instance, if the course content is assessing the antiwar protests of the late 1960s, it is easy enough to find news photos of relevant events (for example, the Kent State shootings). But it is just as easy to also find relevant album art from the times. A search online for sixties art posters not only immediately produces a number of sites with highly relevant images that could be downloaded, but some of the Web sites have good general descriptions of the relevance of the art itself, its political message from 1965 through 1970. For well-known Western artworks such as those by Picasso, Michelangelo, Warhol, and so on, brief online investigation produces the art gallery that owns the work and most often an enlargeable picture of the work, which can be printed. Of course libraries also have art books with images of famous works.

What if you know very little about art history? In any major bookstore, there are numerous books specifically designed to quickly give the reader the feel for any artistic time frame. All one has to do while teaching James or Confucius or Dickinson or St. Augustine or Freud or Seneca or Dante is find the couple pages that describe their culture and times through a summary with images. What was invented or discovered, what wars were raging, and most important, who were the leading artists and what did their works look like and stand for?

The point about bringing visual art into the classroom is that it breaks up the lecture in an exciting visual way that can uniquely advance the course content. The professor who regularly brings in artwork to demonstrate points creates a ongoing parallel "lecture" that widens the impact of the primary material for students while providing relief from regular lecture.

FILMS (NOT MOVIES!)

Showing films for relief of lecture is a ubiquitous practice, and there is nothing wrong with it if films are used correctly and judiciously. First, a professor does not show movies, he or she shows films. Films are shown in classrooms, movies are enjoyed on dates. So a professor does not report to his or her chair that the class "watched a movie today." Rather, "screened a film today" sounds much more like the professor is working hard and deserves a merit raise. The reason why this is worth saying is that you need to be very clear upon self-reflection why you are showing the film. Is it because "it would make the students happy to see a movie in class and they would think I am a cool teacher?" Is it because "I don't have enough material for today's lecture, so this movie will fill up the time?" Or maybe, "I love this movie, so they will too?" All of these ways of thinking about using a film in a course are also associated with the concept of 'movie as entertainment.' A film is a serious piece of pedagog-ical content (even if it may be humorous) and thinking about it privately or out loud as a movie enables "forgetting" its real purpose in the course.

The biggest mistake that professors make is using too much of a film. Often a three-minute exchange of conversation that is illustrative of the point or dilemma students should consider is embedded in a thirty-minute film segment. What to do? Instead of showing thirty minutes, cue up the three-minute segment and verbally describe the setting for it. The film should not *substitute* for lecture. It should simply break it up by illustrating or under-lining the relevant points also made in lecture. If a half-hour or an hour or even a whole film must be shown, this is fine, but break it up. For example, I often use a thirty-minute segment of *Joy Luck Club* when teaching Aristotle. One day I show half of it, and the next I show the other half. At the end of the first half, students often ask, "What happens next? Does the couple stay together?" In other words, they are looking forward to the next class session and, one would hope, to the ultimate point of that thirty-minute segment of film. Classroom chairs are not made for film viewing, and turning down the lights creates the conditions for the ultimate in hiding behavior—secretly sleeping. Hence it is better to parse out longer films when possible since it creates and maintains interest in the purpose of the film and fights against the monolithic presentation style the introduction of the film was meant to break up. That is, showing a feature-length film is just as one-dimensional as lec-turing for two hours.

Using a couple minutes of film once a week in a course may be easier than it seems. Films do not have to be directly related to the content. A his-tory professor teaching a section on Napoleon might naturally turn to a Napoleonic biopic. But the professor could also show a segment of *A Tale of Two Cities*, based on the Dickens novel, portraying the patriotism, classism, and contradictions in France at that time. A psychology professor in a mod-ule on human memory might show a scene from any number of postmodern movies that explore memory, such as *Memento* in which a man with impaired short-term memory tries to solve a murder. But the psychology professor could also present a film that illustrates a self-induced memory deficit, such as a memory lapse from heavy drinking (*Leaving Las Vegas*) or (in the same film), the burning of family photos (memories). There are films or scenes in films that depict almost any major issue that is discussed in classrooms: race relations, falling in love, greed, instinct, mathematical reasoning, the Renais-sance, tragedies, various communication theories, decision making, human development, and the list goes on.

PERSONAL EXPERIENCE

There are two senses of personal experience here: the student's experience of their person as they sit in the classroom, and the professor's personal life experience. The students can be asked to test out theories and claims as they sit in their seats or to experience the "feel" of some concepts. For some disciplines, such requests can be more easily made. A psychology professor can ask students to examine their perceptions of something in the room or to learn, memorize, or attend in a new way, right then and there. In a module on "personal space," a sociologist might have students try to feel how far their space extends beside them, behind them, and so on. Or in a module on obedience to authority, the professor can challenge them to do something they would not ordinarily do (for example, hop on one foot, go buy a pizza for the class), all under the authority of the professor. Philosophers can ask students to do thought experiments, a standard part of doing philosophy. Theologians or religious studies professors can ask students to do some of the exercises of the various disciplines (control breathing, still the mind, pray, contemplate a koan).

There are other surprising and constructive ways to use personal experience in breaking up a lecture. For example, many disciplines teach some form of critical thinking, either informally for part of a class session or more formally. Some disciplines that include critical thinking in their curriculum are communication arts, literature, philosophy, history, and many of the social sciences. Linking concepts with feeling is one way to break up lecture and make it about personal experience for a couple of moments. For example, coming to a conclusion in a simple deductive argument *feels* different than in an inductive one. One can ask students to feel this difference, and many will. A good correlation feels different than a bad one, and cause and effect feels different than either.

Various disciplines use literature as main texts. The feel of a "stream-of-consciousness" author is different than the feel of another type of writing. When using such a text, a professor can call upon students to introspect for a moment and see if their interior lives are indeed structured as "stream of consciousness." Different types of poetry have different senses of temporality, so they are paced and felt differently by the reader. The professor can ask students, in the middle of the lecture on iambic pentameter, to get a feel for this difference between iambic pentameter and, say, haiku. In using literature, the professor can also call upon the students' imaginations or memory. In the middle of the lecture, in order to reenergize, personalize, and bring down to earth the presentation, students can be asked to empathize or get a feel for the life event under discussion, followed by a silence that lets them try to do it. "Can you *feel* the grief of this character?" Or "Try to remember a moment of intense grief." A biology, psychology, or sociology lecture on nesting behavior can ask students to look at how they have arranged their own bodies and belongings in the classroom.

The point is that appealing to personal experience of students as *embodied* minds in the classroom situation is a way of breaking up the lecture routine that cuts right to the heart of the student—to their person as they are right now in the world. In preparing a lecture, you should think about opportunities to connect the feeling of a living, breathing student with the concepts that are supposed to address a part of that life. In required courses with lots of nonmajors, this is an attempt to connect the inner life of the nonmajor with the life of the discipline you are teaching.

The second sense of personal experience is your own personal life experiences or stories. Everyone knows about students trying to get professors "off-track" by asking about their personal lives or opinions. This is just another way in which students try not to be bored by straight lecture. However, used judiciously, personal stories are impactful learning experiences. As a way to break up lecture, these "sharings" should be short, on topic, and remarkable. They should be short because the course and that day's lesson are not about you. They should be on-topic because class time is valuable, and students should not be charged for self-indulgent irrelevant fluff; this is exactly one of the things for which we mark down a term paper. They should be remarkable because the goal here is to keep the course interesting. Face it, not every little thing that happens in your life is remarkable, so there is no reason to relay it all.

Still, this method of breaking up lectures is vital. Students have a need to know more about who is teaching them, your inspiration, life path, and why you are representing this field of knowledge (even if it is not their major). There is a natural curiosity about the teacher, and it works toward achieving your goals if you use this curiosity to make relevant points now and then. Although it is still the professor talking, it is a break-up of lecture because it departs from the strict presentation of content or textual exegesis, and it is delivered in a different voice. It is very difficult and even unnatural to tell someone about the concept of a heliocentric universe in the same tone and gestures that you would use to recount the story of being awestruck looking through an observatory telescope the first time.

COMFORT BREAKS

In a classroom session that lasts ninety minutes or longer, it is advisable to insert a short break where students may leave the room, make phone calls, and so on. This is at least an unspoken policy at most colleges and universities. A comfort break refreshes the body and mind in obvious ways. As a regular lecture break, it becomes part of the course ritual, and students plan around it. This is great for those that need to use the bathroom often or have little ones at home that need a phone call every hour. A course that lasts ninety minutes should probably get a five-minute break before the one-hour mark, and a two-hour course, one ten-minute break or two five-minute breaks. Fifteen minutes in a row is too long. There is just not that much to do near most classrooms, and many students will increasingly think of a break that long as a misuse of time and poor organization skills on the part of the professor.

The great hidden purpose of the break, however, is social. The students get to know each other more, and they can interact with the professor. Smokers congregate and discuss life (and the course), and seatmates continue conversations interrupted by the beginning of the session. Shy students may take this opportunity to ask the professor some questions one-on-one, and others will also seek you out. You should try to make it a point to hang around and be available, not make phone calls or go back to the office.

Professors tend to make three big mistakes when it comes to breaks. First, they strike a bargain with the students to end class early instead of taking a break. Many times students readily agree to this, especially in a predinner, prerush-hour time period, or in an evening class. The professor is not doing him- or herself any favors here, and the students also suffer. This lack of a break subverts the social aspect of the course, relegating time for students to casually interact one-on-one with each other to before class or after. And since students have not been able to get to know the professor during the breaks, or to hear him or her talking casually with other students, that aspect of the professor's personality gets left behind. Students often bring up content problems or misunderstandings in lecture during the break, and these can be addressed when class resumes. The break is important for the overall classroom experience and should not be foregone.

The second big mistake professors tend to make with breaks is that they try to take up business with a particular student that has a good chance of not being completed by the end of break. This could be very important business, such as explaining why that student got a lower grade than he or she expected on a paper. Such a conversation could easily go ten or fifteen minutes, and a student may simply say "I get it" just to keep the conversation within the five-minute break time. Also, conversations during breaks are very difficult to keep private, so if a student needs to be chastised for consistently being late to class or shows up after being absent for two weeks, the conversation is better taken up after the class than during the break.

The third big mistake is not to resume class on time after the break. Restarting class late changes the class culture so that a five-minute break very soon becomes a ten-minute break. Punctual students resent the teacher and the tardy students, and for good reason. Resuming late also gives students the perception that the course or the professor is unorganized, a frequent question on student ratings forms. Dressing down a student publicly for being late back from break is too unpredictable. You are just as likely to get an "I'm sorry, I had to finish throwing up because I'm sick" as an "I'm sorry, you're right." Talk individually to students who are persistently late back from break (for example, after class). They usually get it. If not, after several come back late on a given day, you can say, "I'm not picking on anyone in particular today, but I will have to cut out the breaks if the class members can't all be back on time, since the lateness is disruptive to learning." They are likely to get the message.

Finally, there are other kinds of physical breaks that are momentary but work wonders to refresh students for a little while near the end of a long day of class. I once observed a class that was two hours and fifteen minutes long, with a ten-minute break at the one-hour mark. But at the two-hour mark, the professor said, "OK, time to take a little stretch." Remarkably, at least to someone who had never witnessed this, about thirty-five of the forty students promptly stood up at their seats and stretched as if they were in the seventh inning of a baseball game. This was not weird to them. It was anticipated and appreciated, since it had been established early in the term and consistently practiced by the professor. It was a well-spent sixty seconds by the professor in order to steel students for the last fifteen minutes of presentation. Another trick, also used by therapists of various sorts, is to tell the students to breathe. "OK, we've twenty minutes left and you've completed this week's classes, so let's all take a deep breath. Go ahead, breathe. There you go . . . [pause] . . . Now let's finish up."

CHAPTER THREE

The Best Discussions and Student Presentations

⸻ ◆ ⸻

Discussions are not just useful for breaking up lecture. They are a main component in better classroom teaching. Even if you did not like discussion-based courses when you were a student, it is now expected that a lecture course will have some formal or informal discussions: students expect it, and administrators expect it. Informal discussions are not strictly task oriented and can be initiated by the students or by the professor. Formal discussions, which are distinctly task oriented, are presented in this chapter. There is a goal to accomplish in the conversation (unlike informal discussions), and they are almost always initiated and designed by the professor. A final section on student presentations (oral reports) completes this chapter since they often involve groups working in small teams.

ARRANGING A DISCUSSION

Not every professor feels comfortable physically arranging a discussion in the classroom, directing students to attend to each other rather than to the front. If you are already a pro at this, you may want to skip this section.

Determine the number of students you want in each group (or team). The more students in a group, the longer the discussion should be. Hence, if your plan is for a short discussion, think in terms of dyads or triads, since these involve the least physical rearrangement. A longer discussion project may have four, five, six, or even on occasion, a simple split of the class into two big groups. Do not overlook the power of the dyad. It is effective and very easy to say, "Now turn to another student in class, one other student, and discuss what Keats means when he says . . ."

Arrange the groups. Take a moment to survey the layout of student seating in the classroom that day. This is especially important when discussions are held early in the course, such as the first or second day of class. As you look around, note natural groupings for the number of students you have in mind. For example, if classroom desks are not fixed to the floor, and if you are looking for groups of three or four students in a class of forty, you will proba- bly be fine by just asking them to arrange themselves in groups of three or four. But keep an eye open for groups that are too large, and direct students to rearrange themselves to make a group of six or seven into two groups.

Some classrooms pose special challenges for arranging the discussion groups. The rooms may have fixed desks or alternatively, chairs at tables that are too large or heavy to move around quickly. The simplest solution is the same for both situations, since students are essentially fixed in place. Have one row turn around and talk to the row behind it, and in the leftover row, if there is one, the middle person in a group of three slides backwards so all three can see each other. For example, imagine a classroom arranged around ten students sitting in each of three horizontal rows. The professor directs the first row to turn around and talk to the second row, "You two [nicely gestur- ing to two first row students] please turn around and talk to you two [second row students]. Thank you." And so on across the first two rows in the room. Then the professor directs the last row by gesturing to groups of three or four to talk together, "The middle persons in each group must move their chairs back a little or lean back so that everyone can see each other in the group."

The verbal instruction on how to arrange is important. You want to con- vey both the limits of group size and permission to be nice to each other. For example, for desired groups of three or four students in a room with movable desks, "Please arrange yourself so that you are in a group with several other students. Be accommodating and help each other out. A group of two is too small, a group of five is fine, but three or four is best. You may have to actu- ally move from where you are." Many students need to be given permission to invite each other into groups and to look to be so invited, so encouraging accommodation ("Help each other out.") is a good idea.

Make sure to request that each group has a scribe. This helps the group focus on producing results and lets the professor gauge the progress of the group by reading over the scribe's shoulder while roaming around the room. Also, if groups are not asked to write (a composite sentence, a list, a defini- tion, etc.) they may falsely believe they have finished the task, but their results are vague without the precision that writing them down demands. A scribe can be self-chosen or assigned by the professor "This time, the scribe is the person in the group closest to the front door of the room." Also, for larger groups and more complicated tasks, it is a good idea to insist that the group has a "tracker." A tracker's role is to gently keep the group on task and make sure that not just one or two persons are doing all the talking.

Some students are comfortable talking in the same group each class ses- sion, yet others feel they are "stuck" in the same group. Hence in arranging group discussions, be aware that having the same students talk to each other all the time in the same groups may cramp learning dynamics and dull otherwise sharp discussion exercises. One way to change it up is by putting the following on the board before a particular session and enforcing it as students file in for class. "For today only, sit where you do not normally sit, and do not sit next to whom you normally sit next to." Then proceed with lecture and discussion as normal, explaining if you like that you have done this to change up for today, at least, discussion partners. Another option is to randomly hand out various prearranged discussion topics on that day's reading, one on each index card, and one index card per student. Then instruct students to find the other three students with their same discussion topic to form a group. Finally, use the roll of students' names to group students in various ways on various days. For example, groups of four students starting with A, B, C, D on one day; groups of four starting with A, Z, B, Y on another day.

A good way to liven up the discussion task for longer discussions is to use the space outside the classroom. Often there are unoccupied rooms on the same building floor or one floor away. There may also be benches in the hallway. Scope these out ahead of time to make sure they are available, then alphabetically call off students in groups of five (or whatever) and watch them leave the room to accomplish their task. But before sending them off, it is wise to have a printed copy of the task for each student to take with them and perhaps to go over the task prior to dismissing them. Give them some idea of the timing for return to the classroom, since there will be at least one group remaining in the room. Why empty the primary room of people leaving behind belongings?

DISCUSSION GOALS

Students are frustrated by pointless discussion exercises, as they should be. Have a goal in mind, and let students know at some point, before or after, what the goal of the discussion is. Discussions are not just useful for breaking up lecture. They can substitute for lecture content; they can be designed to prepare students to do well on a creative or challenging assignment; they can get students "into the head" of the writer they are reading; demonstrate dynamic concepts or principles; and much more.

SUBSTITUTION FOR LECTURE

In some situations it is more fun for students and professors to arrive at an understanding of the material through small-group discussion. These situations include general and specific reviews, critiques, and introductory (background) material. Sometimes the present course builds on knowledge from a previous course, so it requires a general review. For example, a history professor teaching a sophomore-level course might need students to recall the elements, events, and character of the Renaissance as it was introduced in a prerequisite first-year class. Instead of lecturing, which may be very boring for some since it is a review, the professor arranges small discussion groups with the specific goal of creating a list of elements, events, and ideas associated with the Renaissance. After debriefing the groups and emphasizing certain results, the rest of the pertinent content can be filled in with lecture. If all goes well, essentially the same content will be out in the classroom as if the professor presented it. The continuity between parts of the students' education, previous courses, and this course is also underlined, which is always beneficial. The same strategy can be employed for reviews of the material that have been presented in a specific course, such as a review prior to an exam.

Critiques are also amenable to small-group discussion rather than lecture. If students have just read a novel or article, and the goal of part of this class session is to generate a critique of the reading, it is just as easy to have students do it in discussion. Critique does not necessarily involve a lot of background knowledge or technical terminology and mostly rests on being able to summarize the point or argument of the author and gauge its worth or veracity. For example, suppose that in the middle of a module on extinction of tribal customs on the Pacific Northwest coast of the United States, an anthropology professor has had students read an article by an animal behaviorist about how whales should not be hunted, even though this has been the tribes' custom for generations. It may be much more exciting for this professor to turn over the critique to students in small groups and assess what more needs to be said after the groups are debriefed than for the professor to plod though critiquing the article in front of the class. Not every topic is discussion-worthy, but a professor needs to recognize a juicy discussion topic such as this when it presents itself. The students are bound to become much more involved in this topic through discussion than as passive listeners.

Often a course or segment of a course includes introductory reading material that the professor knows is new to the students but will get taken up again in numerous ways later in the course, enhanced, and augmented. This is a great opportunity for using a discussion instead of lecture. Discussion here can achieve the goal of introducing the material because gaps in understanding that remain from the small group discussion will soon get dispelled as the course progresses, as will misunderstandings; and the material itself is not yet replete with difficult technical language and concepts since it is introductory. For example, a philosophy professor wants to introduce students to Socrates' concern with wisdom and virtue, so has students read an early dialogue by Plato. Instead of lecturing through the dialogue, the professor can arrange small groups that bring out Plato's main points. If they miss some points, or if they do not quite understand yet that is fine, since the course includes several longer, more developed Platonic dialogues whose study will rectify any deficiencies.

PREPARING STUDENTS FOR ASSIGNMENTS

When an assignment is unusually creative, challenging, or multifaceted, a professor can use small-group discussion to demystify the expected outcomes of the assignment or to motivate students to start working on it. When used near the date when the assignment is due, students who have "gotten" the assignment can share their work with others who are still struggling with how to start. When used soon after the assignment is unveiled, a well-designed small-group discussion can lead students through part of the process of the assignment, which can be either part of the thinking required to successfully complete it, part of the writing needed, or both.

Following is an example of how small-group discussion can help students do well on challenging or complicated assignments. Suppose a human development professor is teaching psychosocial stage theorist Erik Erikson's "Eight Stages of Man" and wants students to write a paper that creatively reflects on their own lives as if they were now eighty-four, sitting on a porch. This type of assignment calls for a lot of imagination and reflection, since the students must apply the psychosocial concepts to their own (imagined) lives. In addition, suppose the assignment calls for the development of two voices, a story-telling voice recounting the life events and a scholarly developmentalist's voice explaining the stages. This assignment will be challenging even for many juniors and seniors.

What to do? A small-group discussion can be arranged that leads students through the kind of thinking and writing they will have to do in the paper itself. Before arranging discussion groups, perhaps the professor uses in-class writing (see chapter 2), instructing students to reflect on a psychosocial stage they have already passed through, for example, stage 4 "Industry vs. Inferiority," and write down events that might have captured each of these in their preteen and early teen years. After several minutes the professor arranges dyads (which are emotionally safer than larger groups for this more personal discussion). The students are instructed to listen carefully to each other as they tell the story of these childhood events. The discussion can continue to a second stage, or the professor can debrief the class. In debriefing, general observations about the process can be expressed by students, and the professor can respond. The professor can use the experiences of the students to bring out how the second voice and first voice would be differently developed in the paper and how they are related. Students will naturally have questions about style, scope, organization, and so on, that they would not have otherwise been aware of until perhaps too late. And the professor can clarify any vague instructions or criteria that come to light through the discussion exercise. The goal of this discussion is to have students attempt in class the kind of thinking and writing that the assignment calls for and then share this experience of working on the assignment with others. The upshot is that a course can be designed with more challenging and creative assignments if the professor keeps in mind this use of discussion groups, a discussion that asks students to think through one segment of the actual assignment.

Imagine yourself lecturing with unchecked enthusiasm about the genius of a particular thinker or writer. You are beside yourself with excitement about what a certain thinker must have been going through in order to create that great work or make that discovery. The look on the students' faces? Amusement, kindness, confusion. They do not quite get what was so revolutionary about Marcel Duchamp's "Nude Descending a Staircase" or St. Thomas Aquinas' *Summa Theologica* or Harriet Tubman's role in the Underground Railroad. You want nothing more than for the students to feel the intellectual quandary and pain of the previous failures of this great figure, the social and cultural pressures that squeezed that person into becoming an icon in the discipline. A well-designed small-group discussion can create empathy and appreciation by placing students in the position of the figure in question, trying to solve the problems he or she is solving.

I will use Plato's *Republic* as an example, since parts of it are taught in a variety of disciplines, including philosophy, politics, government, classics, education, and history. Students often see Plato's *Republic* as a dated document, unimportant because it is out of touch with modern times. They will say that it is interesting but "not really relevant." After students have read through some of the text, a well-designed small-group discussion invariably shows that most students largely share Plato's assumptions and conclusions about how a city-state (the Republic) should be designed, as well as much else. For instance, almost all self-identified, "politically liberal" students end up agreeing with Plato that some music and "free speech" should be censored!

During the second or third class on the *Republic*, I implement a discussion—incorporation of a city-state—designed to have students follow the intellectual, problem-solving footsteps of Plato. I arrange students into larger groups of seven or so after giving them the following written discussion instructions on a handout:

"DIRECTIONS: With your teammates, record responses detailing what kind of city-state you will have. When finished, you should have something substantial to say about your rulers, laws, police and military, and inter-city-state relations. You will also have a city-state mission statement and a name." The subsequent directions can be more or less detailed. On the rest of the handout, I list the four major things to think about—rulers, laws, military, international relations—along with some provocative questions. For example, under the heading "Rulers," I write, "What kind of person or group should rule and why? Be specific." This entire discussion can easily last an hour. The point is that the students work hard at trying to solve the same problems about people living together as did Plato and end up with a new appreciation for the rest of the *Republic* as they read on.

Another example, this time from art or art history, would be Marcel Duchamp's attempt to capture flowing process, three-dimensional movement on a two-dimensional surface of painting, in "Nude Descending a

Staircase." Before lecturing on the postmodern perceptual challenges to previous concepts of art, the students can be asked, in a well-conceived small discussion group task, to solve the problem or riddle of how to represent three-dimensional movement in a two-dimensional medium. This sets them up to appreciate the problems of representation facing Picasso, Duchamp, and others.

The idea of asking students to identify with the author, artist, leader, hero, or icon is part of a much larger philosophy of learning that asks students to come to the similar or the same conclusions for solutions or actions that the figure came to. This important function of small-group discussion was implicit in the human development assignment above on applying Erik Erikson at age eighty-four in the student's life, namely, an attempt on the part of the professor to have students relate the material to their own lives and beliefs.

DEMONSTRATE DYNAMIC CONCEPTS OR PRINCIPLES

Theories can be tested in real time in the small-group discussion. These types of exercises coordinate with the ones described in chapter 2, in the section on "personal experience," since they ask students to test out theories in person, right there in class. The difference here is the group aspect. In a section of a course in social theory, small discussion groups can try a live test of a particular social theory having to do with verbal behaviors or eye contact. In a section on political theory, larger groups can determine how they will divide up into smaller groups using a certain geopolitical scheme. In a section of a cultural theory course a small group can test a particular theory of "tribe" formation, perhaps with each member having preassigned roles.

There are also commercial games that are specifically designed for use in classrooms, especially geared toward cultural, social, and political studies. Some professors successfully model in-class games after successful TV games such as Wheel of Fortune, Jeopardy, Hollywood Squares, or various Millionaire games or survival scenarios. But beware of the Rube Goldberg lecture trap described in chapter 1. Keep it simple. I knew an English professor who used tic-tac-toe as a regular teaching game in her composition course—easy to set up on the board, and most everyone knows how to play.

DISCUSSION STRUCTURES

Regardless of the goal of the discussion, the structure of the discussion must be carefully devised, and procedures or instructions should be clearly spelled out for students. Unless it is meant to be very short, probably in dyads, make up a discussion sheet for each student with the procedures written out. A paper-saving alternative is to write the procedures on the board if they are simple enough, and have students copy them down into their notebooks. Following are brief descriptions of some types of discussion structures, with their main features and benefits.

A discussion may have two or more connected parts, but the way they are related can vary widely. This second part can represent a coequal goal of the discussion with the first part, such as when the first part asks for a definition, in the students' own words, of a central but notoriously vague and difficult concept that they have recently been introduced to, and the second part asks for the application of the concept in an imagined life event or story. The professor is looking for adequate struggle and response on both fronts, defining the term and applying it. However, the real goal of the discussion could have been simply a very good definition in the first part of the discussion exercise. Perhaps the second step was included in case some student groups finished early, and the professor wanted to further challenge them and keep them occupied while other, slower groups where given a chance to complete the more important task. If so, even students in groups that never got to the second part still have the discussion sheet and may be encouraged to think through a response to that part on their own time. Also, it is possible that the written directions do not include the second part at all but that the professor has already thought ahead about what a second part would be like if needed in this way. When a group is finished early, the professor orally delivers the next set of instructions (as part 2).

Another use of successive parts in discussions is to lead students to one definitive statement about a concept or issue after broad reflection and group discussion. For instance, a discussion could ask students to start with brainstorming in the first part and end with a precise conclusion in the final part. Essentially, the students are guided through a process that winnows down the topic or issue to what is most essential, and they express this essence. For example, imagine that a part of a communications course asks students to differentiate news reporting from editorializing. The professor may set up a discussion in which the students are first instructed to build a list of what is essential to each, in two columns. Only after this are they to construct a complete, informative sentence that definitively distinguishes news reporting from editorializing. A parallel discussion structure involves having students successively (in two separate parts) examine and play the role of proponents on both sides of a contentious issue. The real goal is a final statement (the third part) that represents the consensus of the group on the issue. If no consensus is obtained in a particular group, this result is also pedagogically significant for that group. When arranging discussions this way, it is useful to have students take the more precise, extreme positions. For example, in the communications course instance, the students would (1) defend (by producing a list of written reasons) the view that all news should be objective, not personal opinion, (2) defend the opposite, (3) try to arrive at their own view of the matter. Finally, another possibility is to give students three key concepts that are used by a particular theory or figure and have them arrange these concepts in a new sentence that has minimally twenty words. This task forces students to figure out the relationship between the concepts—hierarchical, causal, disjunctive, and so on—and then successively to report to the rest of the class and hear how others arranged them.

HOME PREPARED

In another sense, a discussion can have two parts when students are asked to prepare some written question or produce something that then becomes the starting point of the discussion. The one-page, daily writing assignment introduced in chapter 4 can be used this way since students already have it with them in class. Students can pass them to other students in the discussion group and create some product relevant to that session's aims. Also, these can be used in dyads by having students read each other's papers and add three more sentences to their partner's paper to continue and deepen the thinking, as described in chapter 2. Or the student can write questions on this paper that the two can then discuss.

Another home-prepared strategy is to ask students to read the assignment with a certain concept or issue in mind and write a sentence that essentially expresses the meaning of that concept to bring to class. A good way to distribute this, say in a class of forty, is to choose eight main concepts, write one concept on five cards, a second concept on the next five cards, and so on, until there are forty cards, eight concepts, in clusters of five cards each. These cards are mixed up and handed out to students before they read the assignment, then they read the assignment and write their sentence on the card. When class convenes on that day, the professor asks students to find others with their same concept. There are now eight groups of five students each, and the professor can give them further instruction, such as, "Each student should read aloud his or her sentence to the others, and through discussion the group as a whole is to come up with and write down one, new, great sentence to share with the class on your topic." A variation is to have some of the different groups work on the same topic, and in debriefing each gets to see what the other group with the same topic produced (that is, have four concepts instead of eight, but still only have groups of five persons). Make sure to collect each student's index card and give credit for the assignment.

TEACHING OTHERS

A discussion can be set up so that a significant part of the goal is for the students of one group to teach the rest of the class what they have produced. The debriefing of the groups by the professor can proceed as usual, but first each group presents its findings to the rest of the class. The presenter plays a key role in this type of discussion. The professor can designate a presenter or leave it for the group to decide. Too often the scribe is also the presenter by default, so he or she does double duty, and if there is a tracker in the group as well, then in a group of five people three jobs are done by two students, while three other students may not have to worry about being very involved in the discussion. This is why I like to give the instruction that there will be a lead presenter from the group assigned later, but it may not be the scribe, so all must know what is going on in the discussion. Usually, students should know ahead of time that the group will be presenting its findings to the rest, since this helps the group focus also on how to communicate its discoveries. Another aspect of students teaching others in the discussion process involves arranging different instructions for different groups. A simple example is when one group tries to put together a brief summary of a reading, and another group creates written notes from a specialized critical perspective (for example, political), another group from another perspective (for example, social welfare), and so on. The result is that each discussion group has publicly contributed to the overall goal for the discussion session by dealing with the material through distinct instructions. One more example of teaching others in discussion is when smaller groups, for example dyads, complete a task and then are combined into larger groups of four. Part of the procedure at the combination will be for the members of each group to teach the others what they produced and why.

FILL IN THE BLANKS

Along with the instructions, students can be asked to fill in the blanks in columns or in a table. Although it sounds very structured, this kind of assignment can really be open-ended. A professor teaching any kind of developmental theory, for example, political, psychological, or social can create a grid with space for students to create a fictional character or country that passes through those stages. As a group, students creatively fill in the blanks demonstrating that they understand the development of the concept. For example, in a political science course, students can demonstrate how a particular political theory stresses the fact that one form of government gives way to another. One benefit of structuring the procedure and information in tables or columns is that the task is straightforwardly organized for students, so they can quickly get into discussion on what content to produce. Another way to use fill-in-the-blanks is to ask students to arrange concepts within a certain given arrangement, for example, a flow chart or a hierarchical clustering, and to explain why they put a particular concept in a particular position.

EXTREMELY UNSTRUCTURED

Discussions can be intentionally unstructured for specialized pedagogical purposes. A metadiscussion, a discussion about discussion groups, is one example. This may be appropriate when reading specialized material in a variety of courses, such as sociology, history, political science, philosophy, education, and communication arts. In this type of discussion, the professor deems it advantageous to let students wallow in their discussion assumptions by giving little or no instruction. The ultimate goal is for the students to reflect on the very process of the discussion. Depending on the course and its content this could be authority, eye contact, emotion, leadership, or social assumptions. Debriefing by the professor here is very important and could usually be preceded beneficially by a second part of the discussion in which students debrief themselves first.

DEBRIEFING

Small-group discussions should be more or less thoroughly debriefed. Debriefing most often means that the professor leads discussion by soliciting and responding to group results or inviting others to respond. The professor's job is to graciously acknowledge the group work, make further observations, make corrections where warranted, concede difficulties or problems in the instructions or group process if evident, and recap the general observations of the class. A good rule of thumb is to allow for debriefing as much as 50 to 75 percent of the original time of the discussion itself. There are exceptions to this, depending on the nature of the discussion goal and its place within the overall lesson plan for the day. Also, debriefing may not be desirable or even possible that same day. For example, the *Republic* discussion described above can easily take an hour, so an hour-and-twenty-minute class session may not see a decent debriefing. This debriefing can be moved to the start of the next class. In the meantime the written results can be posted on the course Web site. In any given debriefing session, students might complain that there was not enough time to finish the instructions or that the results were ambiguous or vague. The simplest answer is that class discussions are a moment of a larger process of learning, and this particular discussion is meant to give a beginning of reflection on the topic, not an ending.

STUDENT PRESENTATIONS

Student presentations (oral reports) can be the most rewarding part of a course for both the student and the professor. A student presentation is an assignment in which the student does independent research, often as part of a team, and then orally presents the results to the rest of the class. The assignment should also have a written component. This account is a segue for chapter 4 on assignments since presentations are assignments that usually involve discussion in small groups.

Why have an oral presentation at all? Almost every human being must orally present to small or large groups at some point in their lives. These occasions may be quite regular, such as for a salesperson, a manager, or a teacher. But even a solitary worker may find him- or herself having to give a toast to three hundred people at a wedding reception. The oral tradition predates the written tradition and is still very much alive in our contemporary society. In some way or another, every college mission statement says it is preparing leaders, and it follows reasonably that leaders must be able to give a speech to followers when called upon. When mission statements appear at the school or departmental level, they are often very clear about educating the student in terms of oral and written skills. If you are using student presentations in your course, find the justification for making students orally present in front of others, and briefly write it up as part of the rationale for the assignment or as part of the syllabus.

There are also several practical reasons for considering student presentations. An upper-level course may be run well as a kind of seminar in which each student presents a part of the reading to the rest of the class. In effect, they are teaching assistants or seminar leaders for a day. A skills course, such as a critical thinking–oriented course, may have a significant part of the course dedicated to learning skills and the rest dedicated toward applying it to some topic area. This application could be through student presentations. Also, a course that is essentially both theory and practice is ideal for student presentations. For example, an applied ethics course differs from an ethical theory course in just this way. In addition to some work on theory, an applied ethics course should involve modules on any issue from genetic engineering to cannibalism. The professor could choose some topic and hope that all students will be interested. But much more can be accomplished pedagogically with student presentations. Each student chooses a topic and researches this topic in detail. So the student learns it and writes about it and writes about someone else's presentation (this is discussed below). This way students apply the theory themselves, witness their peers do the same, and are exposed to numerous topics in the field.

The knock against student presentations is that they are low-quality products. Since students are not teachers or sometimes not good students, a course chock-full of student presentations has diminished quality. I believe this is true unless certain teaching strategies are successfully put into place.

The student presentation assignment should have five basic components: a media-rich oral component; a self-reflective written component; a second written component, which is a critique/analysis of another's presentation; a specific audience participation component; and a step-by-step completion guide with deadlines. In addition, if the assignment represents a significant portion of course time and worth, it should involve at least one face-to-face sit-down meeting with the professor and should have the status of a special event in the course.

The actual presentation by the student should have some media component. This can be a prop, a chart, PowerPoint, overhead transparency, white or blackboard, video, song, and so on. This forces the student into doing something beyond just memorizing index cards and standing there presenting information. Using media will also be expected in many future career presentations. In addition to the way it opens up the physical presentation, requiring media often means that the student is forced to think about the audience in a way that requires deeper reflection. In other words, requiring media increases the possibility of widening the scope of that student's learning and application and will more likely make the presentation better, more interesting, and possibly more fun for presenter and audience.

The written self-reflective component of the presentation encourages attention to the group dynamics (in team presentations) and the student's role in it. The student is asked throughout the process to keep a record or log of time spent, with whom, doing what. This forms the basis for a more formal self-report that the student hands in at the end of the project, attaching a copy of the actual log. Following is an example of a handout for such a purpose. It is an otherwise mostly blank sheet of paper titled "Personal Diary of My Involvement" with the following instructions at the top of the page: "LOG: What went on in the group *today* from your own point of view? Note date of entry, approximate amount of time spent, how communicated (for example, person to person, email, or telephone), what you did, which of your contributions were accepted, which were turned down, thoughts about the group process, problems, etc. The professor should be notified if there are persistent problems in the group process." Each student is usually able to use this one sheet of paper to record all participation (each student has a sheet). Later, this log is attached as back-up evidence to the self-reflective form that is equally simple. The self-reflective form (along with the log) gives the professor an added context for grading the student's overall success in the assignment. One model for a self-reflective form in student presentations is to simply put two statements evenly spaced on the page, so students can respond using this sheet of paper: "From my perspective: What I did well in this assignment" and "From my perspective: What I could have done better."

A second written component—a critique/analysis of another's presentation—doubles the topics that each student learns about, lets students get their own grades for a part of the assignment (not a group grade), helps ensure good audience participation and attention, and creates cross-communication among students within the course. As part of the assignment, each student has to write a short paper (for example, seven hundred to one thousand words) on some other group's topic, also taking into account that group's actual presentation. This amount of research is not as deep as the original research into the group topic, and students are encouraged to share materials and knowledge with others who come asking when writing on that group's topic. So each student learns about a secondary topic of personal interest and gets graded specifically on his or her work within the overall assignment (not as part of a group). This encourages students to be attentive and take notes on all the presentations since they may not know exactly which one they will write on.

Audience participation should be mandated. That is, students should get credit for learning how to be critical listeners. Especially in more introductory courses, students may not ask questions or make points in lecture because they do not know how. Student presentations are an opportunity to teach students how to be active audience members, how to ask respectful, but probing questions, or how to make points that extend what the speaker is saying. So there should be a portion of each presentation that is reserved for student questions. For example, a two-person team may have a fifteen-minute presentation in which they are not to be questioned until their formal presentation is over (not to exceed ten minutes), which leaves five minutes for questions. Students are instructed how to ask questions or make points, and the professor actually models this for them and may step in, stopping the action to do so. There are proper and improper ways to pose questions or make points in academia as well as in business, and these moments in the course are dynamic and fun for the professor and students. Associating grades with each student's individual participation as an audience member also means that students take notes and pay attention to the content being presented. That is, it helps active learning.

A step-by-step completion guide with deadlines keeps students on track and guards against last-minute, slapped-together presentations. It will not eliminate bad presentations, but it will reduce their number. The following are some official deadlined events: pick topic/teammate preferences, first team meeting, submit bibliography, submit outline, meet with professor. The professor can aid the process at the beginning by giving students a list of possible topics. The first formal group or team meeting, when team members first meet as a team, should probably be a part of the class session. An outline deadline could be incorporated into the meeting with the professor and used as focal content in that meeting. The other written material (self-reflection and writing on another topic) can be handed in at the end of the term.

In sum, successful student presentation assignments are more likely to involve media, a self-reflective writing component, a written critique of another group presentation, an audience participation component, and a guide with deadlines. Two more strategies are recommended.

First, since preparation is largely independently accomplished, and since it is a major part of the course, the student presentations should also involve at least one face-to-face sit-down meeting with the professor. Each student in the course gets to know the professor up close and personal, which is encouraged by most institutions as "personal attention to student learning." Such a meeting includes an outline because this ensures the group has done some prior work even if the outline is significantly revised. The professor can instantly see which groups are prepared and which are not and intervene. The professor can deal with troubles in the group dynamics that may not have otherwise surfaced but that could fester.

Second, if the professor has allotted a significant portion of course time and worth to student presentations then they should be treated as a special event. On presentation day, some students will take it upon themselves to make the presentation a formal or a fun event, dressing up or otherwise playing roles,

and the professor should lightly encourage this. When I used student presentations in teaching an undergraduate evening course in critical thinking, I called
the event "The Stars Come Out at Night." A number of students became quite
engaged in the theatrical feeling of presenting to their fellow students in the
evening and treated it as a special event, both fun and formal at the same time.
Pedagogically, it helped many students to become more involved with the
assignment emotionally than they otherwise might have been.

CHAPTER FOUR

The Art of Assignments

------- • ◆ • -------

In many ways, assignments make or break a course. In most lecture courses, completing reading and writing assignments is all that students do, in addition to showing up for classes. Assignments are not rest stops. They are not just an assessment of what is learned in a course as if the course were pulling over to a rest stop to kick the tires and enjoy the view. Assignments are highways of learning. Well-crafted assignments make teaching more fun and grading less painful.

ASSIGN READINGS SMARTLY

Assigning daily or weekly course readings may sound like a no-brainer, yet the amount of reading and the timing within the course can be tricky. Naturally, more difficult readings should be shorter in page numbers, and easier readings should be longer. It is also acceptable for the reading assignments to be ahead of class lectures. For example, you may want to pull concepts from deeper into the reading into the present day's lecture without having to formally present that future reading right now. Having students read behind the lecture may be acceptable in certain circumstances, such as when students are facing a very difficult text, but this is less common. If the text is that difficult, it may not be worthwhile.

Do the course readings start in the right place and build upon each other? Do they hang together in a coherent way? This is less of a problem for professors using one textbook for a course, although they may still have to make wise decisions about which part of the text to use and which to leave out and in what order to read. For other courses, the order of the readings takes a lot of thoughtfulness. For instance, suppose I were to take an interdisciplinary approach to a required core course on the philosophy of human nature (a core course found at most Catholic institutions and all Jesuit universities). I could conceivably use a Toni Morrison novel, a very difficult, short, philosophy book by Jean-Paul Sartre, an autobiography by a schizophrenic, a long Hindu poem, and a brain-based account of personality. I have no trouble drawing a philosophical line through these diverse readings (I have used all of these books before), yet I am faced with the problem of coherency in reading assignments for this course. The book I choose to start with frames the course for students. The book I choose to end with can cement my view of the matter. Also, major assignments need to be placed smartly as students are in the midst of completing reading assignments. For example, a novel is easier to relate to and easier to read, hence should it come first to capture students' attention? Or should it be placed after the midterm exam as midcourse relief and rejuvenation? The point is that for many courses, the order and timing of the readings matters. The professor's own interpretations of the material enter into this decision and should show through.

GET STUDENTS TO READ

If a significant number of students are not coming prepared to class, it is the fault of the professor. Teachers who whine that students are not prepared for class, that they are not doing the reading, that they are not coming to class with assignments in hand do not deserve sympathy. A course design should assure that students do the assigned reading. There are traditionally two ways to do this. The first way is to require some sort of extra assignment linked to the daily reading. The second is to arrange, promote, or frame readings so that they make sense, are inherently interesting, and students actually look forward to completing the assignment. Using both together is very effective.

Professors successfully link an extra assignment to the daily reading assignment in a variety of ways, written or oral pop quizzes, very brief papers, diaries, and so on. The keys to success here include some penalty for failing to read or failing to read well (no credit), some real value in course standing for completing the extra assignments (credit), and integration into the learning goals of the course. If there is no penalty and no real value for their final course grades, a sizeable percentage of students will irregularly complete the reading assignments. So, for example, having students write a one-page paper on the reading once a week might be worth from 5 to 20 percent of the course value, perhaps mixed in with attendance and actual in-class participation. The carrot and the stick are the same thing here and are usually effective. Note that in a class of forty students, there will sometimes be one student who does not want to "participate" in any way other than writing the major assignments. No carrot, stick, or reasoning will change his or her mind.

The pedagogical goals of the course should influence when and the mode in which students execute the extra assignment that goes along with the reading assignment. For most lecture courses, the professor needs students to have read the material *before* the lecture. However, it is possible that for very difficult material, reading after the lecture is better. In either case, professors often direct the reading and response to the reading with "thought questions" or other specific directions. In courses that stress critical thinking, however, this may not be a good idea since recognizing a thesis and what supports it, or separating out the central ideas from what is peripheral, is part of being able to think critically. If the professor does this for the student then this learning goal can be subverted. What if the unguided student hands in a one-page "reaction" to the reading and gets it wrong? Exactly! This is corrected directly in responding to the writing or indirectly in lecture and is called "learning."

The goals of the course should also influence the mode of execution of the extra assignment. For example, in courses that stress oral communication, public leadership, or similar skills, the most appropriate extra assignment mode may be surprise oral quizzes on the reading at the beginning of class. Several students are asked in turn about various facets of the reading. If one of the main goals of a course is to enable students to simplify larger domains of knowledge and summarize or reinterpret it for others who do not have technical familiarity with these domains, for example in some types of education courses, the assignment may be to summarize the reading in a set number of words. In courses designed to get students to think and write for themselves in a critical way, such as in many courses in philosophy, literature, history, and communication arts, the assignment should go beyond a summary and demand the development of written critical thinking skills. Hence such an assignment might ask the student to take a stand on the reading and argue for this point of view.

I would recommend a "credit" or "no credit" notation, written at the top of the one-page paper or quiz. A number system is more complicated than the assignment requires and slows grading. A check mark at the top is simple but impersonal and conveys that the professor barely read the paper. If a student is heading down the wrong path in fulfilling the requirements but has actually done the work, a warning credit with an asterisk ("credit*") lets you explain at the bottom of the paper next to an asterisk how it is going off-track.

EXAMS

Most courses should have one major in-class written midterm exam, likely an essay exam that lasts around an hour and tests students' understanding of the readings and lectures. A course should have a good exam because it rewards engaged students and exposes disengaged ones in a way that no other instrument can do. Practically, it also takes less time to grade than papers since exams are shorter, comments are minimal, and the dominant mode of attention in reading an essay exam is "what is missing" (which usually trumps some overall grand assessment of the writing, a dominant attention mode in papers).

Exams generally reward those students who actually takes notes, are prepared each day, and are actively taking the course seriously. For instance, Wendy may never take notes, hardly does the reading, and misses key days of class (the sunny Fridays), but she may be an excellent writer and ace the papers assigned. Meanwhile, Jon is not a naturally gifted writer but takes all the facets of the course seriously. Since an in-class exam should target the students' understanding of what the lectures and readings have been about, and what has actually transpired in class, Jon is likely to shine on this major assignment, and Wendy is not. This is how it should be. In the end, Jon and Wendy may get the same final course grade, yet this would be unlikely without a weighted midterm exam.

In larger classes, professors sometimes are unsure if the student handing in the work is doing the work. Ghost writers for student papers are an old tradition and more common than we would like to think. An in-class exam can help confirm or disconfirm the professor's suspicions about a particular student's work. Sam writes sparkling papers on Shakespeare but does not seem to get Shakespeare in class sessions. In the Shakespeare exam, he cannot put together a paragraph that is factually correct or otherwise on target. Sam's work bears closer scrutiny after the exam. Is he cheating on paper assignments? Does he have a learning disability?

What does a good essay exam look like? By "essay exam" I mean an exam that requires students to formulate discursive writing in response to a prompt (a question). It may be short essays, such as a paragraph, longer essays, or a combination of both. A good essay exam includes clear instructions, good timing, relevancy to material studied, high expectations, and room for the student's own perspectives.

CLEAR INSTRUCTIONS

Make instructions and the prompt as precise as possible. This may include giving away some of the answer as a clue to get students immediately headed on the right track. Do not worry about giving away the store. A student that has no fiscal plan in the first place will not know what to do with the couple of dollars inherited as a clue. The biggest mistakes professors make are ambiguity and vagueness. Ambiguity is when a prompt has both a desired meaning and an undesired meaning at the same time. Students interpret this as a "tricky question" and hold the professor responsible for their problems with the exam.

Ambiguous Prompt: For Plato's *Symposium*, what does Socrates' interaction with the main character tell us about beauty?

Disambiguated Prompt: For Plato's *Symposium*, what does Socrates' interaction with Diotima tell us about all human desires and their relationship to beauty?

The "main character" could have also referred to Alcibiades or Agathon and "about beauty" could have referred to Socrates' own personal preferences, the Greek ideal, or Socrates' well-known ugliness. Vagueness is when a prompt is not well-defined.

> Vague Prompt: Describe any one of the four arguments in Plato's Phaedo. State the overall point of that argument.

> Precise Prompt: For Plato's Phaedo, describe in as much detail as you can any one of Socrates' four main arguments (cyclical, recollection, affinity, or causation). State the overall point of the argument with respect to the dialogue as a whole.

The Phaedo has many arguments and some main arguments that overlap, so the precise prompt gives exactly the four in question. This prompt also now tells students to give full detail in description and tells them exactly what to do with the "overall point of the argument." By the way, giving the students this clue that names the four arguments is not giving them much at all. If they have not been paying attention in class, and if they have not studied, they will fail to adequately respond to this prompt.

GOOD TIMING

Good timing means placed well within the course development, and it means rightly anticipating how much time is needed to complete the exam. As professors teaching nonmajors, we must use many complementary methods to engage students with our discipline, including assessment. Only having an in-class exam at the end of the term means that disengaged students have not yet felt the sting of being disengaged. For the final exam, they may scramble, borrow notes, but the learning experience will not be as rich as if they had gotten the wake-up call half-way through the term. Obviously, an exam too early in the term is not as worthwhile, since there is less course development so far. There is a reason why students and professors call them "midterms." Set the time limit for the exam so that an average, well-prepared student can reasonably finish the exam in the time allotted. Sitting for two hours and writing in class is too long for undergraduates. Ninety minutes is about the maximum a professor should ask for. In the traditional scenario, these are rough drafts created on the spot, and the return on investment wanes quickly after about seventy-five minutes. Most of all do not design an exam so that only very few students will finish it. What could be the purpose of this? Fast writing should not be so obvious a part of the criteria for good performance. Be sure to unobtrusively count down the minutes remaining on the board for students.

RELEVANCY TO MATERIAL STUDIED

Students rightly complain when a test is unexpectedly different than the material they studied. Trying to be tricky or purposely elusive is foolish. The purpose of the exam is to see if students get it, to see if they have been understanding the classroom events, lectures, discussions, and readings. Why try to trip them up? Sometimes students think the exam does not match the material because they mistakenly prepared wrongly for the exam. You need to be clear about how to prepare for the exam and what will be covered by it. Therefore some professors give students a simple study guide that contains a variety of "possible" exam questions, telling students they will choose some from these for the actual exam. If lots of material is to be covered, this is a good practice.

What most professors do not do is tell students exactly what to do with the study guide—namely, pretest themselves. Here are instructions for pretesting, a version of which should be handed out to students for any major exam and should definitely be a part of a study guide:

Pretesting

For timed exams, pretesting yourself is the best method for improving your exam performance in any class and for making more efficient use of limited study time. Following is a description of how to do this.

1. *Study* until you think you know it well.
2. *Create* a testlike setting: a quiet room, a clock, blank paper, and pen, no open book or notes. Note the time and give yourself a time limit (for example, fifteen minutes or thirty minutes, etc.).
3. *Start* by writing a response to a major question in the study guide. Continue writing until you feel you have written everything that has some significance in relation to the issue, or until time has run out.
4. *Leave* it alone for a while, at least five minutes or longer.
5. *Read* what you have written and have your book and notes available.
6. *Analyze* or *evaluate* the strengths and weaknesses of your response. What did you know well, and what did you miss? Does your essay emphasize what was emphasized in class? Have you named key terms and defined key terms in your own words?
7. *Study* again the parts of the material that you feel unsure about. If none, then move on.
8. *Repeat* the whole process until you feel you have the best understanding of that issue or text that you can have or repeat with another main issue.

The benefits of pretesting are time efficiency in studying and less test-day anxiety. Students who pretest do not have to waste time studying what the exercise shows they already know, and they can target what it shows they do not yet know well. It also is a form of practice, which helps alleviate performance anxiety for many. If it is an open book or open notebook exam, the student can bring this pretesting material to the exam.

HIGH EXPECTATIONS

A well-designed exam tests whether students understood what was going on in class sessions, so it involves some memorization, for example, of definitions or events in a story. But this should not be all the exam is about. The exam should challenge students. It should ask them to provide fresh examples, to put major concepts into their own words, and allow room for the student's own perspectives. Memorizing notes or readings is only a baseline in understanding. It is mimicry. Genuine understanding comes through application and interpretation. That is, an exam should ask the students to show they have reflected on the course material and mastered what it means. Following is an exam prompt on Plato's *Republic* and *Apology* that asks students to do these things. (A version of this prompt originated for me with Dr. Francis Ambrosio in the late 1980s and has been improved upon recently by Seattle University professors, especially Dr. Paul Kidder, in working on various assessments of student writing.)

Challenging Long Essay Prompt

Write an essay according to the following instructions. In your essay, take the instructions as an opportunity to show your understanding of the author's argument and a detailed familiarity with the assigned texts. For Plato, a major part of understanding what it means to be a human being in a society is explained by what might be called philosophical education. Do the following:

1. Write a well-organized essay that discusses in detail how the Allegory of the Cave in the *Republic* illustrates and helps develop Plato's concept of 'philosophical education.'
2. Indicate how the Allegory advances Socrates' philosophical viewpoint of education as described in the *Apology*.
3. Formulate a reasoned objection that you, or another philosopher who disagreed with Plato, could make to Plato's claims about the nature of a human being in society.
4. Comment on the relevance or irrelevance of Plato's philosophical point of view for our times.

This also could have been written as one question with several parts, but they are separated out for clarity. Parts 1 and 2 are somewhat difficult, but studying notes and memorizing can greatly help students here. Part 2 does ask for some synthesis that classroom lecture provided only in outline. Notice that part 3 will really separate out the As from the Bs from the Cs. This is the most challenging part of the exam, and it demonstrates well how this prompt is relevant to the whole enterprise of the course and is not just memorization. Like many other courses, philosophy courses are interested in teaching students critical thinking, as requested by part 3, and assessing value of various concepts for daily life, as requested by part 4. Note that additional instructions tell students how each question is relatively weighted: "There are four related questions. Question 1 is *most* important, question 2 is *second* in importance, 3 is *third*, and question 4 is least important. But *all* are important."

PAPERS

In an average lecture class, the paper assignment and its grading are the most personal interaction you have with the largest number of students (all of them). Each student does what you instruct and waits to hear back for your assessment. Therefore, paper assignments demand a lot of thought. Well-designed paper assignments include clear instructions, creative or challenging elements, written criteria, appropriate length, and relevance to course material.

CLEAR INSTRUCTIONS

Paper instructions should be written not oral, whether posted online or handed out hard copy. Oral instructions for papers should only be used as addendums to written instructions, perhaps in response to student questioning or to further explain in lecture how to succeed in the paper. The instructions should have a brief justification for the assignment if possible. For instance, a simple compare-and-contrast paper assignment of two historical figures might frame the reason for choosing the compare-and-contrast approach. In a psychology course, the instructions for a compare-and-contrast paper assignment of Sigmund Freud and Carl Jung might start with, "We have seen how Freud contrasted his own theory of the unconscious with Jung, and vice-versa. Now it is your turn to enter the discussion." In a philosophy course, a paper assignment that calls for students studying Plato to write in dialogue form may state, "With Socrates' daily discussions, and Plato's written dialogues, philosophy began as a lively exchange of ideas between two or more personalities. As beginning philosophers, you will create a philosophical dialogue in your own style."

Truly major assignments, which means papers that are worth 20 percent or more of a course grade, should probably have more structured instructions than papers worth less. Major paper assignments can still be creative, but creativity should only be a facet of the paper criteria. For major paper assignments at the 100, 200, and 300 level, think in terms of a paper that has similarities to a take-home exam—a kind of hybrid between a take-home exam and a creative paper. For example, assigning a paper worth 30 percent of the course grade, with little instruction about how to proceed, may work for seniors, but even that is not guaranteed. Why invite the hassle that comes with a student misunderstanding the instructions unnecessarily, when you can clearly ask for exactly what you want? One way to achieve clarity is to break down the assignment for students, let them know how much to write about a certain issue or author. For example, if the Freud-Jung paper is a five- to seven-page paper, the professor can recommend the following breakdown for students: "Each of the following should equal about *one* page of the whole, either as a block of content or organically intermixed: Freud on Freud (his own opinion about his own work), Jung on Jung, Freud on Jung, Jung on Freud, and you on Jung and Freud." As is, this paper assignment is very straightforward and perhaps dull, but the student has a clear idea on how much writing to devote to each thinker.

Creative or Challenging Elements

Papers that challenge students or require them to be creative are more fun to write and more fun to read. They can also be a wonderfully dynamic exercise of course goals. A central question for the professor in assigning any major paper to students should be, How do I give students the opportunity, within the scope of the assignment and course goals, to be genuinely creative? Seri- ously considering this question is crucial to job satisfaction. The professor may have to read twenty, forty, or one hundred or more of these *same* assign- ments in a short span of time. If well-constructed, reading all these papers will not be such a chore. A meaningful, creative element in the assignment gives each paper the potential to be unique. And this is the other side of the coin. Each student now has the opportunity to be bold, to shine, to impress the professor in his or her own way, showing a bit of personality and values. Of course, not all students will rise to the occasion, but most will try hard for a good professor in a well-designed course. Opportunities to be creative may not arise within the students' own major courses, consequently, creative assignments are a special pathway to engaging nonmajors.

Two main ways to make an assignment creative or challenging are to either reinvent the format of the paper or make the paper personal. In the Freud-Jung paper example, one could reinvent the format of the standard compare-contrast arrangement and make it a dialogue (or play) with these two figures as the main characters. Notice that the amount of pages or words dedicated to each portion of the content can be the same: one page for Freud on Freud, one page for Freud on Jung, and so on. Even more creative is to sug- gest students make up their own characters to stand in for the two great fig- ures, just so the paper makes it clear who is who (for example, a student might name a character "Oedipus" for the Freudian side). Other format reinven- tions are possible with this same example. The student can be the ace reporter "coming live from the DPN (Depth Psychology Network) studios," reporting on the historic confrontation between Freud and Jung. Again the proportional content is the same as with the standard paper. Or students can be asked to write a diary from the point of view of a patient seeing both Freud and Jung. (Some caveats should be put in place that the paper is not meant to be actually therapeutic for the student, only pedagogically relevant.) As a student, which paper would you look forward to writing, with just the right amount of anxiety to feel challenged? As a professor, which paper would your rather read—a hundred times?

The format of a standard paper can also be reinvented to strengthen student writing and thinking. For example, students in entry-level courses that stress arguments or critical thinking on social issues often hold contradictory positions simultaneously. They do not see the positions as contradictory because they are not attending to the implications of the two positions. One way to bring this to their attention in a standard position paper assignment is to force students into a format that highlights the implications of their position. For example, after a thesis statement, the students are directed to spend the rest of the first page developing the implications of the position. This is challenging for most students and extremely difficult for some. Imagine a three-page position paper assignment on whether the 1954 United Nations Charter has an incurable Western bias. After introducing the paper assignment, the next part of the instructions might look something like this:

> For PAGE 1, paragraph 1: This paragraph will be a very short statement of your thesis.

> PAGE 2, paragraph 2 (or the rest of page one, but not significantly more): The rest of this page will articulate the implications that follow if your thesis is right. What is the significance of your position should you be right? (I realize that implications naturally come last, but we put it here for reasons explained in class, namely, to take the opportunity to emphasize how "buying into" a position entails ramifications.)

As mentioned in the previous section, notice the clear instructions about what to put where. The instructions that follow would tell students to dedicate pages 2 and 3 to arguments for their thesis. The point is that by reinventing the position paper into this odd format, putting the implications right after the thesis instead of putting the arguments there, the implications are intensely highlighted, and the paper is more challenging and more interesting to try to write.

Major assignments can also be reformatted in creative ways to take advantage of today's dynamic forms of media, yet without sacrificing rigor. For example, in a course that uses parts of films to dramatize points of lecture or for class discussion, an otherwise dull assignment can be reformatted to include film. Various theorists a course might focus on make claims about politics, business, relationships, incarceration, gender differences, social or personal development, or culture wars; the list is endless, as is the list of films students can analyze and interpret to explain the theories, arrange the concepts, define the terms, and so on, all of which a professor might otherwise ask them to do in a standard paper. For example, sometimes when teaching Aristotle's ethics, which is about how to develop good character over a lifetime, I take a standard assignment that asks students to define and explain Aristotle's main concepts and remake it into a film-based assignment. Students must find any film that depicts character development (most do) and use the film as fodder while explaining Aristotle's ethics. An anthropology course might stress theories of cultural difference, and an assignment could incorporate film into the mix, including documentaries. In addition to film, assignments can be reformatted to include music (lyrics), poetry, or Web sites. A lot depends on the media interests of the professor.

In addition to changing the format, a second main way the professor can make the paper more creative and challenging is by making it personal. This means asking students to think for themselves and take a stand. As mentioned above, this is also a strategy for making exams more pertinent and challenging. The original version of the Freud-Jung paper mentioned above mandated at least one page to the students' own take on the controversy. But the reinventions of the format discussed above have called out the students' personalities in other ways as well. The Erik Erikson assignment mentioned previously—sitting on a porch reflecting back on life as an eighty-four-year-old person—is also challenging because it is personal. One of the conditions of the assignment is that it asks students to reflect on their lives even if the students choose to fictionalize the aims and goals of their lives (few will choose to do this).

WRITTEN CRITERIA

No professor wants to encourage a debate with an angry student concerning what was actually said aloud in class about paper criteria. As part of the written instructions, a paper should have written criteria. If these criteria are well written (and well applied), they allow the professor to justify grading when students question a particular grade. Also, in the moments preceding when papers are handed back, a general review of the assignment goals and criteria can be recapped aloud.

The written criteria can be anything from a simple check list of what should be included, to a complete rubric of all the grade levels. A simple way to present criteria is to state what the better papers will look like. The following is the criteria section of a position paper assignment: "*Criteria:* The better papers will clearly state their thesis and develop it in an organized way, anticipate and develop possible objections to the point of view expressed, and attempt to overcome those objections. The better papers will also be reflective. Yet, to illustrate and ground the reflection, they will use the principles, events, and characters of the books and the concepts presented in class, where appropriate." Notice how the criteria link the paper assignment to the text and to what went on in class sessions. Very creative paper assignments should list "creativity" or "originality" as part of the criteria. It would be unusual for this criteria to be the most important, however, since making good arguments, or demonstrating understanding of a thinker, text, or theory, or some other more easily demonstrable skill is the required writing goal in most required courses for nonmajors (except creative writing, of course). Also, in almost any course "creativity" or "originality" in writing and thinking is a legitimate criteria for an assignment since most disciplines and even university mission statements profess to value them. On a particular paper, it is often appropriate to tell students exactly which criteria are most heavily weighted. For example, a list of five criteria for a paper might state that the criteria are listed in order from most important to least important, but all are important. Some professors also list general criteria for all papers in the course syllabus (for example, "All papers should have no more than one grammar mistake for every 700 words"), which can then be amended or particularized as assignments are actually administered.

PAPER LENGTH

Within their major, students should learn to write longer papers by the time they are seniors. Hence it is not unusual for senior synthesis courses to expect a twenty-page paper or more in addition to an oral report and other work in the course. However, most professors teach courses where nonmajors predominate as well, for example, as part of the core requirements of a liberal arts degree or as part of corequirements (art majors taking a philosophy of art course, criminal studies majors taking an introduction to psychology course). So how many pages should a paper assignment require? As few pages as necessary to get the job done.

Requiring a six-page paper in undergraduates classes when a three-page paper will get the job done does not make any sense. A shorter paper makes the student practice how to write concisely rather than practice how to fill up pages with tangents. A shorter paper gives the professor more time to attend individually to each paper and more time to personalize comments. A paper worth 25 percent of a course grade can be a three- to four-page paper (1000–1400 words) if the assignment is well designed. A paper worth significantly more (for example 40 percent) would likely cover more material and have to be longer. Also, clearly set a minimum and maximum number of pages ("minimum three full pages, maximum four pages," "full pages" meaning that a two-and-one-quarter page paper is not adequate). Setting a maximum discourages the student mentality that "writing more means a higher grade" when it really just means that they have written more, and you have to read more. Keep the range of pages tight; notice that a three- to five-page length requirement for an assignment may have the professor comparing a student paper that is three pages to one that is 66 percent longer.

GRADING

Since criteria differ for various assignments, the grading also differs. By grading I mean not just the number or letter grade, but also the written feedback the professor gives. For in-class exams, such feedback is usually minimal as mentioned above. The student either understood the material, or did not. Also, for many final papers or final exams, feedback is minimal since students tend not to pick up the finals. Paper assignments, especially creative or personalized ones, deserve a different kind of personalized feedback.

Often professors will write something at the end of a paper or exam and put a letter grade or just put a letter grade after making marginal comments throughout the writing. One model for feedback on major paper assignments is to make it formal and personalized by addressing the student by name and including a message about the paper. So in addition to a number and/or letter grade, and marginalia by the professor in the appropriate places, the student has a personalized recap. The recap should say what went well in the paper and how it fit the criteria, how it could be improved, or how it missed some of the criteria. "Juanita, your overall point about the intertwining of politics and tribal history in East Timor is a good one. The thesis is clearly stated. The paper could be more effective by choosing better examples for illustration, as I have noted. Also, the argument about Western interventionism and the rise of Islamic fundamentalist policies is not yet well developed. Still, fine job overall." The comments do not have to be long, just efficient.

On papers where students might expose their dreams or aspirations, such as the "when I'm eighty-four" Erik Erikson assignment discussed above, the professor must be firm on criteria and gentle on commenting on the student's personal goals. On papers that call for students to take a chance creatively, for example to write a play or dialogue that they have never before attempted, the professor must acknowledge the attempt to be creative, even when the result is not very good. "Derek, this paper shows sparks of creativity, for example with the elephant metaphor, even if the paper itself does not yet reach full flame." Also, writing grades on the first page for all to see is crude and accomplishes nothing. An A student may be embarrassed by the big "A" emblazoned on the front of the paper, and a D student may take the big "D" as a badge. Not knowing the personality of all your students in full detail means that grading should be a discreet, last-page message to that student.

Using a numbered grading system for the course, and assigning number grades on each assignment in addition to letter grades gives the professor valuable flexibility. Not all assignment failures are the same, so flexibility is handy when a good student honestly misunderstands an assignment and fails it. Suppose an otherwise good student has severely misunderstood the in-class exam questions or has simply frozen up intellectuality from anxiety. Later when the professor discovers that the exam is an obvious "F," would it be fair to give that one good student another opportunity, while not giving other students the same opportunity to improve their scores? The same scenario could happen on a paper assignment. Yet with a number system, the professor has built-in flexibility. For example, if the exam is worth 200 points out of a 1,000-point course (20 percent of the course), the professor can assign a level of failure that indicates the student did *something*, just not something very good. In short, the type of failure matters. The student could receive a score of 40 points, 80 points or 115 points—all "Fs" but very different in the scheme of the course as a whole.

One of the most agonizing tasks for many professors is "adding up" a student's performance over a term to determine the final course grade. Some students are easily pegged as outstanding or mediocre. But facing a list of letter grades garnered by a particular student throughout the term is spongier than getting a solid final number to work with. In a course worth 1,000 points total, a student may have achieved 822. It is immediately evident to the student as well as to the professor that this course grade is a B–. No conversion is necessary from sheer letter grades to numbers or from letters to a 4.0 system. By the way, a 1,000-point course system is intuitively simple and lets the professor *and* the student easily figure out where the student stands, and it translates immediately into weight percentages for segments of the course. If class participation is worth 10 percent of the course, then it is out of 100 points; a midterm exam is 25 percent of the course or 250 points, and so on.

Handing out assignments and handing them back after grading are important moments in the life of the classroom. When an assignment is first handed out, or after students have been given a chance to see it online, the professor should dedicate some in-class time to going over the assignment and fielding questions. Later, handing back the graded assignment incites anticipation and anxiety for most students *and* professors. The key is to take one's time and not rush it. It may have been several weeks since students have handed in the assignment, so make time to refresh them on the task and the criteria. Put information on the board if you need to. Tell them what *you* learned from their research, reflection, and writing. Thank them for their hard work! If a student has a simple question about his or her paper after class, answer it if you can. If it is really a grade complaint, arrange a time to meet with the student more formally and get a copy of the graded assignment ahead of time.

DISTINCTION AND CONTINUITY IN ASSIGNMENTS

Assignment types should differ over the term of the course, and there should
be some sense of pedagogical connection or continuity as well. The distinction between types of assignments gives any one particular student a chance
to express him- or herself in a variety of ways appropriate to the discipline
and results in a more well-rounded appreciation of how scholars in that discipline handle, exhibit, and communicate their knowledge. For example,
anthropology can involve statistical analysis as well as collecting and syn-
thesizing interviews. So a relatively introductory course in anthropology
may want to "test" students in a variety of expressive modes, which might
include orally and aurally, in line with appreciation of cultural oral tradi-
tions. The point is that a course with two in-class exams and no papers
should have very good reasoning for no papers. Likewise, a course should
have very good justification for no exams. More subtly, each major assignment should be differentiated from the other so that a truly outstanding (A)
student is truly outstanding across the board, having consistently been
superb in a variety of assessment instruments. This means that if a course is
designed to have three papers in addition to an in-class exam, the papers
should be differentiated in style and criteria. For example, one paper might
be very creative (and worth a bit less), another may stress the research and
reporting style in that discipline, and a third may be purposely open-ended
to let the student test his or her own interests and voice. Having all the
papers the same, such as all research papers, is unimaginative and is a skewed
assessment of student learning for many courses.

There should be a pedagogical justifiable connection between assignments. This continuity should take into account the expected, increasing
development of student learning in the course. There are many ways to do
this. Some courses are arranged so that students mainly work on one project,
yet that project is broken down into several major phases, each of which is
graded. For example, a course project that is designed to end in a long paper
(written alone by the student) and a group presentation will have a number
of deadlines and checklists that lead the student deeper and deeper into the
final product, from outline and initial group meeting to paper and presentation. Another sense of continuity is the development of skills in a skills
course or the development of concepts in a theoretically oriented course. The
assignments are designed to introduce the next level of difficulty the student
is expected to master—skill or theory or both.

In other courses the continuity is not so obvious, so it should be
explained to students. For example, a professor could assign daily, less formal, one-page "reflections" on the reading as described above, as a way of
easing students into the more formal assignments. Since these more formal
assignments, such as midterm papers, are worth much more, the one-pagers
act as feeder assignments for the major assignments. By the time the major

assignments are asking students to reflect and write on the reading, they have already practiced doing so and received feedback. This preparation is a justification for the one-page weekly writing assignment, a justification students can appreciate, even though the students have to write often. The overall point is that the professor needs to reflect deeply on the purpose of assignments in the course and strive for variety and continuity, so the course is organized and so assignments genuinely help drive the pedagogical aims of the course.

CHAPTER FIVE

Sensible Policies

---•◆•---

Classroom policies and problems are often related. This chapter dis-cusses classroom policies, stated and unstated, including a special sec-tion on plagiarism. The next chapter discusses problems that can arise with students and professors.

THINK DEEPLY ABOUT A GOOD SYLLABUS

Your classroom policies start with the syllabus, so it should harmonize with the general ethos of your institution, its rhythm, culture, and the habits of life on your campus. Still, it is more personalized than this ethos. The syl-labus is a kind of legalistic agreement between students and the professor. Many problems such as attendance, lateness, plagiarism, and assignment issues include the syllabus at some point. For example, when you are propos-ing to your chair how you are going to handle a certain plagiarism case, your chair will naturally ask you what your syllabus says about plagiarism. Study other professors' syllabi in your own department, especially for the course you are also teaching. Many departments keep these on file. If not, most pro-fessors are happy to share. If there is a suggested or generic syllabus for an introductory course, be sure to use it only as a guideline (if possible) so that your own syllabus accentuates what you do well and directly addresses poli-cies that matter most to you.

Surprisingly, many veterans of teaching do not know how to create a clear, informative, well-balanced syllabus. Look at the syllabi from various places. My experience, and my guess, is that they are not easy to read. A good syllabus should be attractive, with consistent style, plenty of white space, and sensible fonts and formatting. For example, would you submit a paper to a journal with italics, bolding, and underlining? If we ask our students for one-inch margins on their papers, our syllabus should have one-inch margins.

Sections of the syllabus should be separated from each other in an organized way. Information should be complete where appropriate, for example, ISBN for books or specific editions that will be used. And information should be left vague where appropriate. For example, there is no reason to include the criteria for the midterm exam yet if it will also be handed out later in the term. A well-balanced syllabus has a statement on plagiarism, but the plagiarism statement does not comprise 75 percent of the syllabus (I have seen this).

How many syllabi in your department actually say what will be achieved in the course in a measurable way, as an outcome? Of course, most syllabi include a brief description of the objectives of the course, but students should know exactly what skill or understanding they will attain. Somewhere in the brief description of the course on the first page of the syllabus should be a statement such as the following, from an upper-level required ethics course for nonmajors: "Upon successful course completion, the student will be able to critically read and adequately respond in writing to a variety of philosophical texts on ethics, and discern the scope and value of the main arguments the author makes. The student will be able to assess orally and in writing the advantages and disadvantages of virtue, duty, and utilitarian ethics." This kind of statement is radically different than just an annotated listing of what books are going to be read and in what order. It is also an outcome measured through the various assignments during the term.

A good syllabus indicates the grading scale for the course and perhaps for individual assignments if that is appropriate. But it definitely should break down the percentage that each assignment contributes to the whole course, for example, "class participation = 10 percent." A good syllabus tells students how to get in touch with the professor and when. It relays attendance and lateness policies and possibly also policies on computer use or recording in class, and includes a schedule of class sessions with a list of readings due for each session.

Finally, a good syllabus very carefully addresses plagiarism. There are various schools of thought on what to say. Rather than take an all-or-none stand, such as automatically failing plagiarists, I advise a more flexible statement. It might be best to indicate to students that plagiarism is an incredibly serious transgression and refer students to the reigning policy book for student behavior. Statements such as "A student who plagiarizes will automatically fail the course" may be justified for the course or the institution, but it leaves the professor and the student very little room for judgment calls. The professor may want to treat a particular case with mitigation, and the student who is facing an all-or-none decision may take an unusually hardened position and fight, lie, cheat, or steal to avoid this sure-fire fate once accused. Here is a statement I currently use in my syllabi: "All quoted or paraphrased material, or borrowed ideas, must be cited or noted as such in written papers. This includes online material. 'Unintentional' plagiarism is still plagiarism. Consequences of ignoring this standard scholarship rule are *very serious*. Also, presenting written work from other students as your own is a serious breach of academic honesty. If there are any questions about what constitutes plagiarism, consult the professor or see our university's *Student Bulletin of Information*." This gets the point across but allows some wriggle room if necessary, as described below in the plagiarism section.

ATTENDANCE AND LATENESS

If you ask around in your department and at your institution, you may be surprised to find a huge variation in attendance policies. Each professor must do what he or she is most comfortable with. But a good rule of thumb when teaching required courses for students regardless of their major is to make regular attendance mandatory. Since the institution is making the course mandatory, not just for majors but for everyone, attendance should probably be mandatory as well. Also, generally speaking, a mandatory attendance policy aligns well with the concept of scholarly discipline that most institutions want to teach. The key word is *discipline*—commitment to a discipline. A required history course may not be a course in the major for a literature student, but chances are scholars in the two disciplines see them as crucially interrelated at some level. That is, requiring attendance supports the bigger picture of liberal arts and sciences as forming a "core," a "requirement" for becoming an advanced, disciplined scholar, no matter the student's major.

Mandatory attendance means absences factor into the grade and that absenteeism could mean a lowered grade or failing the class. Mandatory attendance does not necessarily mean that a student who misses a couple of classes in a normal quarter or semester term will automatically suffer grade adjustment. Following is an attendance policy I use in my syllabus in required courses for nonmajors: "Since this is a core course, diligent class attendance is expected. There are legitimate reasons for being absent from class (sickness, personal trauma, etc.). *It is the student's responsibility to inform the professor about the absence prior to or closely after its occurrence*. Frequent absence from class, legitimate or illegitimate, constitutes absenteeism. *Absenteeism will lower one's course grade, and may result in failure*. Missing three or more classes puts you in danger of absenteeism. If you anticipate missing class because you are a student-athlete, you must identify yourself to the professor early in the course." Notice that I ask students to contact me if they are absent. This is another way to be "available" as a professor, another way to have more interaction with students and more of a chance to get to know them in order to teach well. More important, should a situation become difficult for the student, I am able to follow it along the way to give the benefit of the doubt rather than first hearing from the student after he or she has been missing for two weeks. If students simply show up after having been missing, I point to the syllabus and ask them why they were silent. Also, I inform students that even legitimate absences, such as long hospital stays, can be deemed absenteeism. If justified, as in this case,

I may give the student a grade of "incomplete" for the course and require certain work to be completed once healthy. All of this is in discussion with the student. The "missing three or more classes" phrase changes depending on how many sessions there are in a particular term.

Do not expect other professors to support your attendance policy or to act likewise. A student's morning class may have a professor with a mandatory attendance policy, and this student's afternoon class in the same discipline never takes attendance and does not give it weight in the course. In my opinion, this latter practice is a sort of quietism, a failure to find a way to hold students responsible for their education and take appropriate action when they fail to be engaged. It suggests that nothing important and necessary to their education in this course happens in the classroom. Therefore, you must justify your own attendance policy in your own terms. If you cannot justify why you have a mandatory attendance policy (or the opposite), then you should not have one. The same goes with lateness to class (professors being late is another form of quietism and disrespect for students who arrive on time and pay good money for the course).

With this in mind, I will share my justification for my relatively strict attendance and lateness policy. It was formulated in response to a trend I saw in the secondary student ratings form. Some students complained that attendance should not be required. Hence, in addition to the statement above in my syllabus, within the first two weeks of the course, I send out the following justification of the attendance policy by email (if it is not already part of the course notebook described in chapter 1), along with some similar possible objections to course policy. This type of devil's advocate format is actually a teaching tool as well since it is crucial to critical thinking in many disciplines.

Possible Student Objection: "Attendance should not be required, since we're adults and we are responsible for choosing to come to class or not. And lateness is also our own business. There should be no penalties for attendance or lateness."

Sven's Response: This is a core course, so attendance is required. Lateness is disruptive to learning. In the same way that this course is required for you to graduate, attendance is required for you to pass this course. That is, passing the core courses are a requirement of the degree, and one of the stated expectations of this core course is that students attend the course. Below is from the Academic Policies section, in the *University Bulletin*, p. 50: "Attendance is an essential and intrinsic element of the education process. In any course in which attendance is necessary to the achievement of the course objectives, it may be a valid consideration in determining students' grades." Attendance is necessary to the achievement of the course objectives as listed in the syllabus. Hence part of my job is to note attendance and grade accordingly. The course objectives are achieved through in-class interactions: in-class student questioning, in-class lecturing and demonstration, in-class group discussions and exercises. Therefore, absenteeism subverts achievement of course objectives and lowers one's grade.

I no longer trend attendance policy complaints in any particular term. Notice that the university rulebook does not directly enforce my decision on mandatory attendance. Nonetheless, it can be used as support. Each professor should seek out the official statement on attendance that governs his or her school or discipline. Following is the justification I use for monitoring lateness: "Persistent lateness in a classroom setting is rude, disruptive, and almost always fixable. Lateness disrupts learning by unnecessarily distracting and often physically disturbing other students who have been on time. Some students will be late once or twice during a term, but being late more often at the beginning of a class or after a break is persistent lateness. Such disruption works against the student's own learning as well as against other students, and the goals of the professor and the course, hence it lowers one's grade." Some schools do not allow sufficient time between classes, or some students arrange their schedules in impossible ways. Yet it has been my experience that determined students, once talked to privately about their creeping customary lateness, can and will change their habit.

COMMUNICATION

When I ask students the first day of class, "What do you expect from the professor in a class like this? What kind of things do you need?" one of their overwhelming responses is availability. They want to be able to talk to me when they need me. But how should we communicate? The answer is, almost any way we can. Your institutional expectations for teaching, as highlighted by some question on your student ratings form, is for you to be reasonably available to students for consultations and help.

OFFICE HOURS

Some professors seem to live in their offices, so students always know where to find them, in person or by phone. Of course, these professors also may have to shut down the shop for certain students or at certain times to get things done. This is fine. Even if the culture of your institution is that professors are in their offices when not teaching, this may not have to be your style if it does not fit you. Find out exactly what the expected number of office hours are, and if you will fall short of that, tell your chair why in writing and ask for a response. When you do meet with students in your office, try not to shut the door completely, and if the meeting is likely to be contentious, definitely do not do so, and try to make sure someone else is around, such as a department secretary. I have found meeting with students in my office wonderful and memorable, yet I have never found holding office hours very useful in my career, except for getting to know my office-mates. Office hours convenient to me are not convenient to most of my students, and I work best at my home office. For those, like me, who do not do most of their work in their institutional office, the question is always, "Do students think I am available for them?" I have three main ways of communicating with students—after class, email, phone.

AN AFTER-CLASS STRATEGY

Even if your classes are scheduled back-to-back, and another class pours into your room right after your class session ends, you can still see students after class. This is absolutely the best time to talk to students, other than maybe before class, because both of you are already together. There are two main insights that you need to make. First, most students just need about a minute or so of your time, to ask about an assignment, to clarify something said in class, and so on. Second, you can rightfully carve out time from the end of a class session to meet with students.

Many days no students stop to talk at all, or maybe a "regular" student stays around to walk out with you as you both talk. Some days you get several students who need a word, and rarely, you get a little line-up of students, perhaps six or seven who need to see you. You must deftly separate out the quick questions from the rest. Like a surgery triage, if the student you are now addressing has a quick question, answer it and move on. Invite that student to call or email if he or she has more questions. Students with private or more involved questions are asked to wait. Winnow them down to whoever is left and then move everyone to the hallway, find out who can stay (if you can) and who cannot, and make arrangements. This backup rarely happens. The day before assignments are due or the day they are handed back can be prime days like this. After a normal class, it is a student or two, and questions can be comfortably answered within five minutes, or arrangements for an appointment, email, or phone communication can be made.

The second insight is that you can use the last five minutes of your own class as the most convenient office hours imaginable. This is especially convenient, and I think necessary, when there are tight times between room assignments, either for you to get to your next class or for the next professor and students who need to set up in your classroom or both. When your class ends at 3:20, and the next class starts at 3:30, it is very difficult to legitimately and regularly hold onto the classroom for a student meeting until 3:25. Also, if you have to go to another building to teach at 3:30, it is again difficult to be available to students until 3:25 and be on time for your next class. The solution is to "end" your class early, at 3:15 and use the last five minutes of actual class time to consult with students who have questions. This is reasonable, I think, because of the institution's timing constraints on classroom use along with the requirement to be available to students and because you are using class time to discuss class issues. It is an open, voluntary, small discussion group with the professor, or it is a brief one-on-one with the professor about course content. Within the constraints of the physical schedule and classroom space juggling, you allow students the opportunity for personal contact with you, exactly what the institutionalized criteria of student ratings "availability" asks for. Five minutes does not hurt course content, and in fact, it is equivalent to the open lecture question "Does anyone have any questions about today's class, or about the assignment?" Also, numerous professors on any particular campus routinely let students out of class early—a poor practice, I think, because the students' class time is paid for and set institution-wide. The practice of "ending" five minutes early for the purpose of making yourself immediately and readily available does not negate students getting what they paid for ("immediately and readily" does not mean ending class and then reaching for your books and packing up!).

One need not carve out this five minutes if no other class is coming to use your room and if you do not immediately teach another course. But if another class is heading into your room, say at 3:30, the main problem is that they will come in as other students are leaving. They may see that all the other students have left and that the professor is standing up front talking to one student. The next professor may even come in, if he or she is an early bird. You simply explain to them what you are doing: "My class ends at 3:20, but I end five minutes early, so I can use the time for students, before you all come in. It's 3:17. You may always come in a minute or so after 3:20." The bad news is that you may have to do this several times. The good news is that it is always the same students waiting for the next class, and they learn quickly and spread the word. Once, after repeated interruptions, I had to address the next class (in the hallway! "Can I have your attention, please . . ."), even as the professor came walking up at the tail end of my explanation. I remained undisturbed the rest of the term. Since it is your class time you are using, you are on solid ground with this next professor and next class.

PHONE

More professors now give out their home phone numbers, and some even let students call them on their cell phones. Some questions are best handled on the phone. For example, a student will email me a rambling question, and instead of writing a long response, I ask the student to call me and give my number in the email. In my syllabus I give students my home number, which I call my "home office number," and I tell them to call anytime between 8:00 a.m. and 8:00 p.m., including weekends. In the student ratings, and in the secondary student ratings instrument, students note that including this home number *and* making the weekends available is incredibly valuable. Very few students choose to contact me this way, but almost all are very impressed by my availability, so much so that I almost never get a complaint from students about my minimal office hours. The students who do use it, use it once for an "emergency question" on an assignment or may use it once for each assignment. But because of email availability, and after-class availability, I get a lot of mileage and usefulness out of giving out my home phone, and it does not cost much in terms of privacy. I cannot remember a time when a student called outside of the twelve-hour window or otherwise abused the privilege.

EMAIL

Of all the ways to communicate with students, email is the most effective and useful. Of course, a whole class can be addressed through email, which I do about once a week. This information is about some schedule update or is a link to something mentioned in class but off-loaded to email. But for one-on-one communication at any time of day or night, email cannot be beat. I am careful to rarely answer email outside of the twelve-hour window I give students for phone calls. But I am also careful to answer emails right away. I tend not to handle course assignments or papers through email, reserving it for communication. I tell students that I will get back to them usually within half a day, which is not difficult. They report that they immensely appreciate this response time.

COURSE WEB SITES

What is it that you want your course Web site to do? In the liberal arts and sciences, a course Web site can be valuable. It can give students a central place for links to pertinent tools, such as discipline-specific glossaries or reference styles, biographies of famous figures in your discipline, links to sample papers, the syllabus, and so on. Also, the professor can off-load information that cannot be covered in class, special quotes or further readings, other pertinent Web sites, photos, music, definitions—the list is endless. This off-loading can be planned, or it can be spontaneous. An example of a planned off-loading is when you post FAQ about an assignment on the Web site; an example of a spontaneous off-loading of course content is when a student asks a complicated but important question in a class session, and you promise in class to post a response for everyone to read later that day.

This latter example brings up an intriguing possibility for course Web sites that I have exploited in my classes. A main section of the course Web site can become a parallel, developing conversation in addition to class conversation. The course Web site can have a main section devoted to dated entries from the professor. Not quite a blog (Web log), it is simply a dated list of messages from you to the students that starts from the first day of class when you post a "welcome to the course" message. Once a week or so after that, you post useful, new messages to the class. Directing them, reminding them, adding to class content, and amplifying on policies. It is best to keep to the fashion of the medium, and be brief in your missives. I also email the very same messages to each student after I have posted them, if the message is particularly timely or important. My understanding is that "chat" sessions or bulletin board postings have mixed success and require a lot of work to monitor. But devised well, they could be great communication assets to classroom teaching.

PLAGIARISM

Since plagiarism is a problem that requires a policy, it could go in this chapter or the next on policies. I treat it here as both.

There is no joy in discovering a case of plagiarism. But how it is handled is of utmost importance. Dr. Paul Kidder once gave me the best advice about plagiarism cases. He said, "There is no rush to make a decision, to inform the student, to give a penalty. You are in charge of how this goes, and what happens when it happens. Take your time and go step by step." Sound advice. So what are the steps?

The first step is to know your institution's written, official plagiarism policy. Confronting the student is decidedly not your first step. Doing so could quickly lead you into actions and statements you are not prepared to make and greatly increases the possibility of everything going very badly. Most institutions have recently updated their plagiarism policy. See what students are officially told in writing in the student code of conduct or student handbook. Also, inquire unofficially how others handle plagiarism cases, such as from your chair and other trusted colleagues.

The second step is to make a copy of the work in question. It is helpful if you have not marked the original up yet. That is, when you suspect a student of plagiarism, stop grading and stop marking up the paper. Set it aside, and make a copy to work on. When you have straightforward evidence, you can go back to the original and mark it in a way that a superior (chair or dean) can easily follow to understand the plagiarism.

Third, determine very carefully how strong your case is against this student. Deeply suspecting a student has plagiarized a paper, but lacking any hard proof, is not the same as identifying which Web site the student cut and pasted the information from, for example. In the latter case, you can print off the Web page, attach it to the original, circle the same passages on the original, and the student is caught red-handed. You may have a student who has marginal skills in speaking or writing English yet hands in polished papers. You deeply suspect that the student is plagiarizing or otherwise is not the main author of her own paper. What are your options? Perhaps the student is from a family where the ethos is that if you cannot do a job you pay someone to do it for you, and this is what perfectly respectable people do. How are you going to get past the student to that source and prove that the student has presented this work as her own? In my opinion, you cannot do this well without the student's help and admission. You should definitely talk to the student, point out the anomaly, and ask for an explanation. But unless the student admits to the help, or is not very good at hiding the subterfuge, the only thing you can do (after probing in discussions with the student) is to grade this student more strictly in the future, that is, not give her the benefit of the doubt in grading. This is one reason to link assignments very closely to class content and to include an in-class exam in the course as described in chapter 4. The former trips up the lazy plagiarist, and the latter may help readjust the course grade of a successful plagiarist, assuming he has not also cheated (or honestly studied) for the exam.

The point is that there are two main ways of proceeding in a plagiarism discussion with a student, depending on what the evidence is. One way is, "I have caught you and now we're going to talk about it." This should only happen if you have hard proof linking the source and the plagiarist. The other way the conversation goes is, "I have some questions about your paper," which is really a fishing expedition. This probing is designed not to be accusatory, just in case the student is innocent.

Suppose you have discovered a plagiarist, and you can prove it. If you are an adjunct or even a tenure-track professor, you should inform the chair. Let her know how you will proceed. Keep her in the loop so that the responsibility is spread and a record is established because the case may become difficult. The chair is busy and does not need a detailed account of the situation, so let her know you have caught a plagiarist and will talk to the student in a day or two. And after it is done, let her know briefly how it went and what you did. Keep it simple and professional. Before you talk to the student, mark up the paper copy to show the plagiarism and have firmly in mind what the punishment should be.

Finally, talk to the student. You could talk to the student before papers are handed back. But often this is logistically difficult, and who knows how the forewarned student might disrupt the important ritual of handing back papers. Another option I like better is to go ahead and return the papers, and when the paperless student approaches you after class, ask him nicely to stick around because you want to talk to him about the paper. Do not give any other information. Do not be drawn into a conversation in public. "What's wrong? Why didn't I get my paper back?" Do not take the bait. Most students will know what is wrong and will ask once and then simply wait for you quietly. If you and the student are not able to meet right away for the discussion, then set a meeting. "OK, I can meet at that time, but what is it about the paper?" Your response, "I just want to talk with you about it when we have the time to do so, I will not do that until we meet." Do not take the bait. You need this meeting to go your way, on your terms, in your time frame.

In the meeting ask the student if he has anything he wants to say about the paper. Even our court system recognizes the value of admitting guilt and stating contrition. Give the student a chance to do this. He made a horrible decision and in all likelihood regrets it deeply. In this meeting the student is not your enemy. He is most likely a very embarrassed, very nervous human being. His world right now is jumbled with various ominous possibilities and thoughts: he hopes his parents do not find out; he is worried about his future career, his permanent record, his peers, friends, counselors. The student might also be angry, at himself and at you. Present the evidence and tell him what the punishment will be. Also, make sure to inform him who will know. For example, it may not be the case that the chair of his own department will know, or the dean, if the student is from another major. If not, let him know that you have made the decision not to inform his chair but that your chair (your boss) has been informed. That is, the student should not get the impression that the only persons who know are you two. There must be some sense of authority beyond the professor in case this student gets wild ideas about manipulating the facts and the truth. But the student should also not be led to believe that everyone in the school knows. If the student will be staying in your class, then you want to make sure that he is welcome in it, so long as he does his own work. That is, put the episode behind you both, once penance is paid. If the student has been treated professionally and with respect, then he will do the same. The main "emotion" you want to convey is disappointment, not anger. The student has let you down as a professor in a course that hopefully is designed so that he wants to impress you. This disappointment is something that can be ameliorated with future work, so it has a kind of hopeful side to it—just what a learning environment needs.

Note that if your syllabus states that a student will fail the course for plagiarism, this boxes in you and the student. Knowing this, the student may become immediately hard-lined and make the situation into a nightmare. Also, not all plagiarisms are the same, and not all students are the same. For example, in my experience, some students from mainland China are genuinely confused on what counts as plagiarism in their first year at a U.S. school. In Confucian aesthetics, imitating well is exactly what is considered beautiful, and children at various levels of the educational system are taught to memorize and repeat knowledge. I am not excusing plagiarism in this case. These students should be punished since information about plagiarism is on the syllabus and has been discussed in class. But a vague statement about serious consequences lets the professor have the wriggle room to treat each case on its own merits (demerits), rather than be tied to a blanket statement that all plagiarists will fail the course. Some might also argue that K–12 education in the United States does a poor job of preparing students to correctly cite passages from other works or paraphrase with attribution. Therefore it is possible that a student has entered your class, even as a junior, and is writing her first major term paper. Again, this student should be punished, but I feel more confident in deciding the matter if I have the ability to design the punishment for the case. If the student appears to be more disturbed that she got caught than that she made a moral miscalculation, then this matters in the punishment.

Generally, I do not fail students for plagiarism, but sometimes I do. They redo the assignment and must accept a lower grade in the course. I tell them what their top course grade will be if they adequately complete the course. For example, in a case of "light" plagiarism, continued A or B work (which is their own) may garner them as high as a C minus, which at my institution is a low grade. For a single case of "heavy" plagiarism, especially if the student is not genuinely contrite, he may pass the course with very good future work. In my mind this means A or B work gets him a D of some sort in the course. If all of this happens early enough in the term, the student may choose to drop the course, which is his prerogative. If your institution does not have a form that is given to the student or your chair, then make sure that the meeting has a written follow-up description of the punishment, for example, by email.

Even assignments that are designed to forestall plagiarism will not necessarily do so. They just make the plagiarism more obvious. The professor inputs to an online search site a sentence or partial sentence from the paper, and there it is on some Web site. Still, creative assignments, tightly linked to class interpretations and presentations, and asking for the student's personal perspectives on the issue discourage plagiarism. Certain types of assignments are "invitations" for those who have a proclivity to plagiarize. There is a huge difference between, on the one hand, "compare-and-contrast" assignments or "summarize and give your opinion of" assignments, and on the other hand, the kind of creative assignments described in chapter 4. These generic assignments are just asking for trouble.

CHAPTER SIX

Professor and Student Problems

—————— ✦ ——————

A student problem is usually also a professor problem. The problems can be mild, such as disinterested students. Or the problem can be severe, as when a student tries to "hijack" a class. This chapter addresses several of the more interesting problems that can arise during a term and offers some advice for handling them. Teaching is a job, and any job has problems and challenges. Keep in mind that many can be resolved, but some have no reasonable solution. Therefore, we just move on to the next batch of students with as clear a head as we can and hope for the best. Also keep in mind that most colleges and universities have teaching and learning centers with resources for professors teaching college students. These resources include everything from small libraries dedicated to college teaching, to personnel who coach and counsel professors. Usually these personnel are themselves professors trained to coach professors and will review syllabi and assignments and even visit your class session. Such counseling is confidential (but ask to make sure).

TEACHING DISINTERESTED STUDENTS

If you teach, you teach disinterested students. Some of us regularly teach classes with more of these kinds of students than other professors, since we teach more of the core classes or required classes that students must take outside of their major. The question is how best to approach the disinterested student? Obviously, the professor must find common ground. If the student ratings reports trend that the class is boring, that it is irrelevant, and so on, then it is likely that the professor has not found common ground with these students. In a large class, finding common ground with a certain small number of students is simply impossible. A small number of students are purposely disinterested in their whole education, more interested in the boy or girl they like in the class, and so on, and no amount of wonderful teaching will get them genuinely involved in your course. So you should keep your expectations realistic. However, there are connections to be made in the lives of most students. How?

Starting the first day of class, a good professor collects and remembers information about particular students. This information can be used through-out the quarter in lecture, written responses to students, and personal com-munication. For example, a student asks a question during lecture, and in your response you use a soccer metaphor because she has told you she is on the soccer team. She is proud to be on the team, so this is not only highly rel-evant to her life, but it respects and acknowledges her achievement all in one lecture response. Why choose an airplane analogy when responding this time to this student athlete? Or again, why not a choose an economic analogy when speaking to a business student, and choose a health analogy when speaking to a nursing student? You could choose a history analogy for either, and it may be successful, yet you should subtly use (but not overuse) the per-sonal information you already know, or that he or she has provided, in order to more actively connect to the student. In general, many courses enroll a variety of majors, and the professor should know which majors are repre-sented in the course. You should make it a point to vary lecture examples throughout the term, with these major disciplines in mind, in order to spread the common ground. Written responses to students and personal communi-cation with them can work the same way.

How do you collect this information used in forming common ground? One way is through conversation during lecture breaks or before or after class. Many students are more than happy to tell you what they are interested in and how accomplished they are. They generally want to impress an authority figure, in this case the professor, and with little prompting will readily tell a bit about themselves. This information also comes through informal written assignments where students themselves are asked to find common ground between the course and their lives or majors. This information gathering can start the first day of class. As do many professors, I ask students to fill out an index card with their name, phone numbers and email addresses, and I ask them to respond to the question, "What do you do?" I leave it at that, and they act confused as if it is a weird question. Nonetheless, they give all sorts of wonderfully revealing answers that I can subtly use later in the course. Of course, many students list their jobs and interests: "I spend time with friends and work thirty hours a week at the corner bistro." But students also write such things as, "I play soccer, study, and am sort of nervous about how hard this course might be," or, "I have a three year old, and I'm a competition ball-room dancer." I review these cards several times during the term, which only takes a couple of minutes, to remind myself how I might connect with cer-tain students whom I seem to be losing or deepen the common ground with other students already involved. This information can also be very useful when a problem student surfaces in the course.

There are other ways of coaxing students into the wonder of your course. Assignments are incredibly important in this respect, as discussed in chapter 4. Are your assignments challenging and creative? Do they call upon the students to relate the material to their lives or their majors? It is just plain wrong to assume that your material will shine through on its own merits, simply because it does for you. You must give it the proper pedagogical grease to help it slide into students' everyday thinking. Also, a professor who is personally interesting, enthusiastic about teaching, and engaging with students will be more likely to motivate students than one who is disengaged.

THE AGGRESSIVE PASSIVE-AGGRESSIVE STUDENT

Some students can be aggressively disinterested. I call them "aggressive passive-aggressive." A paradigmatic example is the student who sits in the back row and openly reads the newspaper during class. This student is not disturbing other students, she has put herself in the back row so as not to be obvious (or involved in the course), and she knows that you know that she is relatively disinterested in the course. Suppose it is a required course outside of her major. As a professor in a far away department, you will not casually interact with this student's major professors in the hallways of the department, inquiring about her behavior in class. You will never be writing a recommendation letter for this student; you will not be her mentor or model. Your class is a hoop she needs to jump through in order to do what she really wants to do, for example, work at a job, develop a career, and make money. Perhaps your class is the last required course she needs to take, and all she needs to do is pass the course. The student knows she is smart enough to get a C, or maybe a B if all goes well, without having to pay respectful attention. What to do? Do you go the laissez-faire route and let each party do his or her own thing?

No. This student believes she is showing respect by quietly showing disrespect for what you are trying to accomplish as a teacher. It may end up that this student is irretrievable, but you need to make an attempt. Why? Because the institution expects you to as a part of your job. You are the teaching authority, and it is up to you to try to find a way to reach each student. Read again your student ratings forms, which reflect what the institution expects. They likely include questions such as: "Did the course or professor challenge you?" and "Did the professor promote active learning?" In addition, this student is a bad model for other students, who may take your inaction as uncaring, as inattention to the course.

Take the time to figure out what attitude you will have with this student. Once more subtle approaches have not worked, such as making in-class, direct eye contact, perhaps accompanied with a disappointing countenance, make an appointment to sit down and talk. Why waste your time? It would be a rare professor who did not already have this aggressive passive-aggressive student in mind. Since she is already there, clean up the assumptions, and square away what you think by directly communicating with the student. "Since you read the paper during class, you seem disinterested in the course. Can you tell me about how you see this course?" You may not get the answer you like; alternatively, the conversation may go very well. In any case, you will use the opportunity to tell the student that reading the paper during class is distracting to you as a professor, subverts her class participation grade, and shows a general disrespect for you as someone who is trying to be professional. Only the most obnoxious student would turn down such a request if it is proffered respectfully, and you have attempted to get to know the student in the meeting. This same scenario could be used for distracting computer use, reading other course texts during class time, sleeping in class (head down, etc.) or obvious daydreaming.

In one of my classes, a talented creative writing major had begun working newspaper crosswords during the fifth week of a required philosophy course. I let the first class pass without confronting the student, hoping it was a one-time affair. After the second class of this behavior, I asked her if she would do such a thing in one of her major courses. She quickly and confidently answered, "No, definitely not." This allowed us to continue a conversation about her attitude toward the class and so on, and it allowed me to suggest a constructive alternative to working crosswords. She had already shown she was bright and took special care to write assignments with flourish. She loved words and loved to write and claimed that doing the crosswords allowed her to occupy her mind if class was slow for her. So I suggested that she replace trivial crosswords with her pen and notebook, using her notebook to write creative "riffs," hopefully about course content. This solution worked and was a compromise on both our parts. She never did another crossword in class, and I did not insist that she take regular notes. This solution allowed her to be independent but comport herself respectfully, and she was invited to be engaged in course content in her own way. One key point about this example is that I had to know something about the student, her major, her love of writing, in order to get what I wanted and sense what she wanted. Also, this knowledge about her allowed me to speak to her more personally, rather than merely as a generic authority figure, and we continued to talk regularly about course content from then on.

THE INTERRUPTER

Ignoring the dedicated interrupter is not an option, which is exactly the point of being an interrupter. In contrast to the aggressive passive-aggressive student, the interrupter wants to be seen and heard. Sometimes also called the "dominator," the interrupter is like a child asking, "Are we there yet?" every five minutes of a long trip. The interrupter destroys the positive atmosphere of the classroom and gets on everyone's nerves, including the professor.

An interrupter can be a friendly, engaged student, who has real concerns about doing well in the course (so is not necessarily a "classroom terrorist"), or it can be an otherwise aloof student whose attention and attendance are spotty. Either way, a lecture-based course needs a modicum of uninterrupted segments for the professor to accomplish his or her goals, and the interrupter destroys presentational continuity. No student has the right to make questions or observations at every turn of topic in a presentation in a large lecture class as if he or she was the only student in it. An interrupter is not the student who asks a good number of penetrating questions, perhaps uncomfortable questions about the discipline or the material. Students may roll their eyes when this (noninterrupter) student raises his or her hand again. But this (noninterrupter) student may actually be a model for the complacent students in the course. By contrast, the interrupter is both maddeningly frequent in addressing the class or the professor and is not at all selective in choosing what to comment on.

Everyone is familiar with the classic picture of the interrupter. The student will interrupt the professor very often with seemingly brilliant observations that are just as often either obvious, inane, or severely off-track. This student may only be peripherally aware of this disruptive behavior. Yet there are many possible manifestations of interrupting. For example, there is the selfish student who has the attitude that "this lecture is my toy, and you can't play with it." This student's modus operandus is to sit up front and imagine that the course lectures are being delivered entirely to him. He adds on to the professor's statements or cracks a relevant joke or makes a pun just loud enough for the professor and maybe several other students to hear. This type of interrupter quickly and loudly answers every question asked, real or rhetorical, and rightly or wrongly. It does not seem to matter. This is his private lecture. To any general question, such as, "How did the reading go for you all?" he will answer first and loudest, and the rest of the students may then shrink from answering. This interrupter will speak for the rest of the class in all matters. Often this is a student who does the work and is engaged in succeeding in the course.

What to do? Bringing the interrupter back into line is tricky. The professor wants to lessen the number of questions or observations and increase their quality. I have found that a friendly meeting is necessary with the student for the classroom dynamics to be reinitiated and restored. This meeting is tricky for several reasons. First, the student may not really be an interrupter, so the professor has to be very sure about the consistency of the behavior before talking to the student. For example, it is easier to determine that a student really is an interrupter by the early middle of a term, whereas trying to pin this label on a student early on is difficult. By the same token, waiting too long ruins the in-class experience for other students and threatens the integrity of the whole course. Second, the professor does not want to turn an interrupter into an aggressive passive-aggressive student (see above) or worse, into a hijacker (see below). Third, the professor likely encourages student participation in the course, through statements in the syllabus and in class activities and therefore must honor that commitment.

The purpose of the meeting is to acknowledge how passionate the student is in his own education, and how best to channel that passion in this particular course. In your life as a professor, there are many students who just do not give a damn and turning off a student who is lively about the subject matter and prepared for class is a crime. So let the student know how much you appreciate his involvement. In this meeting you can enlist this student's help opening up class questioning and discussion by asking him to dial back on his own questions. "I see how you have shown others how to speak up in class, but not everyone is as ready to speak out in large groups, or not right away. For some, it takes them more time to warm up. What do you think about letting the shyer students have the floor too, now that they've seen how you do it?" You are asking this student to be more like a leader, which likely supports how he already sees himself, and you are asking him to take social responsibility for his behavior. Additionally, draw a limit for the student. This limit may mean that you move his questions to a weekly meeting or a quick after-class question and answer session on some days, or email. In most cases, this is not as much work as it sounds since the student will find it almost impossible to do the work necessary to keep track of all the topical associations, questions, and observations that he would have otherwise just been able to blurt out in class. Also, the student wanted the professor's attention and now especially has it in a friendly way and is likely to sit comfortably (and more quietly) in class with that special connection in mind. In sum, you need to acknowledge the student's passion (and intelligence if appropriate) and give him another outlet for his concerns.

THE HIJACKER

A hijacker consistently tries to publicly undermine the authority of the professor. This type of student represents a serious challenge to the integrity of the course and the professional life of the teacher and must be dealt with directly and firmly.

Part of the problem in these cases is that the professor is often the last to know that the student is a hijacker, even if other students and professors in other departments already know. The daily in-class challenges that seem off-track and sometimes oddly personal do not immediately tell a professor that this student is a hijacker. And then what has been going on in a veiled way suddenly crystallizes for the professor after some major incident or other. If the irrelevant, irreverent, and veiled disrespect were contained to just the one student, then it may not be a serious problem. We have all had, or will have, disgruntled students who are not very happy about having to take our course and will let it be known in various ways. But this is not what the hijacker is about. The takeover is gradual, public, and influential, this latter since the hijacker will seek assent from others in the course for his or her view, regardless of what the professor thinks of this view. You might get a genuine hijacker every three or four years in steady teaching, but you must recognize a hijacker when you see him or her in your course. A hijacker is not necessarily a person with contrary views—a minority anarchist view in a political science course, or a Calvinist in an existentialist-oriented philosophy course designed to present the case for human freedom. That is, a hijacker is not a student who consistently but passionately expresses a viewpoint in mostly appropriate ways at appropriate times. A hijacker is also not an interrupter. Unlike the interrupter, the hijacker has an agenda in mind, and it involves you and your course, even if she is only peripherally aware that she has it.

Typical hijacker behavior is when the student actually attempts to persuade the class—before, during, and after a session—that the course or the professor is deeply flawed. Once I was teaching a sophomore introductory philosophy course primarily to nonmajors, and I landed a classic hijacker. At first I liked how he (let us suppose) was unafraid to speak up in class. He seemed genuinely interested in what philosophy was about and questioned critically in the way we ask students to do in this kind of course. Before long, however, he was challenging course policies in class and disregarding the reasoned responses. For example, "Why do we have to take an in-class exam when we've all obviously read this stuff?" The question had already been asked and answered seriously, with appropriate context. The difference in the asking of it this time was that he was not asking me. Sitting near the front of the classroom, he had turned around in the middle of class session and addressed his fellow classmates! I actually let a couple of them respond, but it was disappointing in part because they were intimidated. Then I responded again and moved on. I finally realized what was happening, from this and similar incidents, and knew I had to do something, but I did not know the student's motivation. The student's work was very good, and he was articulate and intelligent. I set up a meeting with him.

Prior to the meeting, I found out his major and asked a professor in that department if he knew the student. For the next fifteen minutes I got example after example of how the student had tortured the professor in his class and how he had dealt with it. (However, there was still too much raw feeling in the professor's recounting of the course and not enough good suggestions on what to do.) After informing my chair that I was going to meet with a problem student, I met the student and asked him what his attitude was toward my course, what the aim of his behavior was, and so on. He was quite surprised by my directness, but I was somewhat desperate. "I don't want to douse your passion for your own education, and perhaps for my course as a part of it, but your fellow students are in a difficult introductory course to a new discipline and need a certain amount of trust in the professor to be successful, and the professor needs to be able to lead with some authority, and what you do in class is not constructive." I then gave examples of how his behavior could erode the trust that students must have in their professor and undermine the necessary authority. I asked, "What is your goal? What is it you are looking to accomplish when you do these things?" The student claimed he did not "mean" to do anything by his antics but recognized my concerns for the integrity of the course and the education of the other students since I kept pressing them. The meeting was contentious and long. The student and I reached some understanding, without admission of fault, and the course proceeded with the student becoming markedly less disruptive but continuing to do good work. The payoff was that other students found their voices in the course, and I could walk into class without a sick feeling in my stomach.

To this day I wince as I recall the whole course. As a class, the students ended up rating the course very positively, but I am convinced that the hijacker knew what he was doing and enjoyed it, as if that part of his education were some kind of experimental playground to see how far he could push professors and the "system." Even though in my real life I would have liked to treat this person differently, in my professional life I had to treat the situation as a learning opportunity and present it that way to him.

The point is that students can be meek as sheep or boisterous as hyenas, but a hijacker is a different kind of animal. He or she must be dealt with directly and honestly, since burying your head in the sand will not work for you or for your other students. As a postscript, another professor in my discipline who had the same student a year later reported that the student had no problems in his course and that he could not stop talking about how much he liked his previous philosophy class. Not everything has an explanation!

THE PAINFULLY SHY STUDENT

There are students who seem to have taken a vow of silence. Like almost all vows humans can make, they will sometimes break it, but only if they have to. Their vow includes not talking to the professor, as well as not talking aloud in class. Not only that, but on assignments designed to reveal a bit about the students' own thinking, an assignment designed to connect with their lives, they are determined to hide, and will produce canned or cliché insights. A painfully shy student may or may not exhibit hiding behaviors: a student does not want to be seen in class or does not want to be considered a part of the class. These students pull down hoods or caps over their heads or sit as far back in the room as possible (even though there are a large number of rows between the last seated student in the class and themselves), and so on. On the contrary, a painfully shy student may sit front and center, no hat. What is essential to know about a painfully shy student is that public communication is painful, the larger the group, the more the pain.

Why should you care? As always, it is your job to try to find a way to educate each student, no matter her learning style or abilities, within reasonable boundaries. As mentioned in chapter 3 on discussions, part of your institution's mission statement probably claims that your institution tries to produce leaders or encourages good leadership. Leaders must be able to communicate publicly when required. This requirement may come from outside, as when a student, now a business manager, must publicly address her team on a matter, according to a memo from the boss. But it may also come from inside, when she has to speak up for herself, and she requires this speaking up of herself. Most liberal arts and sciences institutions are dedicated to educating the whole person, including his or her public voice, and part of the classroom experience is the public voice of each student in the classroom.

What should you do? It is a huge mistake to publicly chide a painfully shy student. "You don't like us? You don't want to talk to us?" If the student in question truly is painfully shy, and not just somewhat modest or generally quiet, then this chiding from an authority figure will not work, will cause more pain, and will alienate the student. While chiding is a mistake, encouraging is not. Keep in mind that repeated "encouraging" becomes chiding. A student can be encouraged to speak in class if a course is designed with small-group work every so often. This is one way to allow a painfully shy student to "score" in class participation, beyond simply attending class. It is extremely unlikely that this student will ever raise her hand in open class. She may even come from a culture or educational training that discourages such behavior. So encouraging students to speak aloud in class should be done carefully, with an "out" available. For example, you may have already determined that you will call on that student to speak in open class in way that does not single out. You call on two other students to answer a question about that day's reading, and then you call on this student. She may respond or may not. But this is legitimate encouragement, by invitation, to speak in class. If the student muddles around in response, then you can allow, "If you'd like to pass on this question, let me know." Other students will be eager to answer and may already have their hands up. "Don't be afraid. We're all friends here" is subtle chiding. It assumes the student is afraid and now has made this a public claim, and it parlays on a falsehood of friendliness between students and between students and the professor, which is unlikely.

Hence it is legitimate for you to call out the painfully shy student if it is done in a truly encouraging way, without chiding. You should arrange the course so that such students still get a chance to talk in smaller groups, especially if classroom participation is part of the course grade. And you should generally create an atmosphere that is welcoming and friendly, with non-dismissive, genuine responses to student questions and observations. You might also tell the student, in response to that student's assignments, to bring the written ideas to voice in class. "Pat, these ideas are first-rate, it would be wonderful for you to sometimes share your thoughts aloud with others in class. Other students could benefit from your questions or observations. Think about it."

SPECIAL NEEDS STUDENTS
ARE NOT PROBLEM STUDENTS

As noted in chapter 1, I once taught a regularly scheduled, upper-level course for nonmajors in which a full 10 percent of the course was autistic. Professors are also expected to teach their discipline to blind students, deaf students, borderline schizophrenics, bipolar students, students with a history of clinical depression, freshly recovering addicts, students with aphasia, apraxia, dyslexia, ADHD, and so on. Many times you will not know their learning disability unless they tell you directly, or you will only know it through other official channels, for example, through a letter received from a learning center on campus. I was not officially told of the autistic students at all, until classes had already begun. I found out about one of them purely by accident, just before my first class session, through some casual conversation with the department secretary. So I was not prepared for the students' behavior on the first day of class. How should one treat special needs students in terms of grading or special compensations in order that the course goes well?

An honest discussion with the students about policies, without probing into their personal lives or afflictions, is definitely recommended. It would be rare for one of these students to want to make the professor a main part of their support system. It would be equally rare for a professor to have that kind of time and dedication, not to mention the expertise. There are professionals on each campus who have this job, as well as the student's parents, counselors, and peer groups. Also, many of these students rely on note takers, other students in your class. Let note takers do their jobs; do not get in between the student and the note taker unless it is warranted. Other good practices are to explain instructions as well as possible and keep to a regular break schedule.

In addition to communication, initiated by the student, or gently initiated by the professor if concerned or at the sign of difficulty, the professor obviously should try to reasonably accommodate the student in a way the makes for a better classroom experience. For example, in the autism example, these students were allowed to tape-record the course (something I never otherwise allow). Also, in small-group discussion exercises, after already forming and instructing the groups, I had to give additional one-on-one instruction to each of these students about the task and other details about the group exercise (they were usually dispersed in different groups). This was all as it should be. However, as described previously, I overcompensated in lecture style and by teaching safely at a distance. My fear, bad assumptions, and general lack of knowledge about autism took me out of "my teaching game." I chose to teach at a distance, lowering my passion and engagement with the students, making for a mediocre classroom experience. I believed I was accommodating my autistic students while superbly teaching my nonautistic students. I had no evidence that my normal teaching style would have failed, yet I chose to teach at a distance. The result is that accommodations must be made, but overcompensation can cause even bigger problems for the majority of the students, perhaps even including those students with special needs.

I believe that grading should be consistent, according to the stated assignment criteria, whether or not a student has a learning disability. This is easy to defend in college education, since students are adults, and the integrity of the course and the college degree the student wins is at stake. It is more judicious to be consistent in grading than to adjust grades according to a student's capacities for doing well. Naturally, the criteria for an assignment and a course must be clearly stated, and the students must be told how they measured up to this criteria. The accommodation here can be in the personalized response to the students that accompanies the grade, not in the grading itself. For example, a dyslexic student may have special trouble with a paper assignment that also includes a grammar component in the criteria. If the professor knows of the student's dyslexia, the response, along with the grade, could take special care with explaining how the paper inadequately satisfied this part of the criteria, rather than simply, "Jeff, the grammar is miserable." In responding to the student's work, this special care is an appropriate accommodation, without watering down the integrity of the course.

You may have an obviously deaf student for which arrangements are made. Be sure to talk to the student directly to ask what professors do that helps and what fails to help. The same goes for blind students, who are less common. Do not be afraid to say "I will not be able to do that for you," for example, if the student is asking for a transcription of each class session provided by the professor. My experience is that in these more severe cases of sensory deficit, the students have a very sophisticated support system in place. For example, each of my completely deaf students over the years has had another person, who is not a member of the class, act as their aide in class. This person was employed by the student or on the student's behalf. It is a fascinating and challenging experience to teach in a packed, small classroom, with an interpreter standing next to you signing the whole time, sharing the front of the classroom each class session. More often, completely deaf students have "court reporter" type help, where what you say is almost instantly typed and displayed on a screen for this student, by the reporter sitting adjacent. There is also a chance that in a classroom of thirty, sixty, or ninety students, you have several students with partial hearing loss. Therefore, some good habits are worth developing. Speak facing the class. For example, do not speak and write on the board at the same time, or if you do, say again what you said once you are finished writing. Some students will lip-read to disambiguate what they only partially hear. This is the case even if they have no hearing disability. When showing films, switch on the captioning. For hearing students, the additional visual effect of the words in the dialogue is more memorable than the dialogue alone, and of course partial-hearing students will be able to follow better.

For students with psychological or social disabilities, the in-class challenges the professor faces are much more interesting. First of all, the professor may not know that a certain student has a certain challenge at all! Ever. Nonetheless the student may exhibit behavior that is odd, but the term ends, and that is that. Second, even if the professor knows the student has a psychological or psychosocial learning disability, such as a history of depression or autism, this is not extremely helpful. These are wide and deep categories of psychological labeling, and one frequently depressed student is not the same as another. For the sake of all students with psychological disabilities, be inwardly compassionate and outwardly professional. As noted above, they are generally not looking to make you a part of their support network, yet kindness, as the manifestation of inward compassion, is accepted by everyone for what it is. Professionalism respects their achievements as adults and does not single them out for undue attention.

CHAPTER SEVEN

Understand and Improve Student Ratings

—————— ✦ ——————

Suppose that with your encouragement, your partner accepts a job in another city, so you decide to leave your tenured position to try to teach in that new city. This happened to my wife and me in 1999 as we moved to Seattle. In terms of academic record, what do I really take with me to the new city? Or suppose your contract is not renewed at your current institution. The chair says, "We're moving in another direction." This also happened to me as an adjunct early in my career. In addition to your scholarly publications, your student ratings are the next most portable and important part of your career. Both are often considered more "objective" than anything else in your portfolio. One is a test of how you have been accepted as a scholar by your peers, and the other is a test of how you have been accepted as a teacher by your students.

Student ratings of the course are your institution's attempt to distill the criteria for what should happen between the professor and the students. The portable and conspicuous part of student ratings is the quantitative score. In order to improve and maintain this score in required liberal arts courses for nonmajors, you should treat each student as a voter and keep the ratings form criteria forefront in mind.

As one might expect, many aspects of the student ratings practice are controversial. Even the name I am using—"student ratings"—is a part of the controversy. At many institutions they are called "student evaluations." But some teachers rightly complain that this moniker expects way too much from the students and the form. First, the form is usually a short form, possibly with some room for comments, but the comments are never mandatory. How can such a simple form be as thorough as the name *evaluation* suggests? Second, the students are not in a position to evaluate the course, only rate it. They are not peers to the teacher, not trained to reflect on how a course is structured, what the pedagogical goals were, and how they were achieved. They are not trained to intelligently report this information on the spot in five to fifteen minutes. A true peer could evaluate a course, perhaps including data from student ratings.

Another obvious controversy is the questionnaire format itself. Certain questions may be biased toward certain kinds of teachers, for example, those who are funny or good-looking may get higher scores on questions that amount to, "Did you like the instructor?" Also there is plenty of research in psychological assessment that can be used to mitigate the veracity of subject reports on testing instruments.

There is also the issue of how they are used. For example, some institutions profess to make them an important part of the teaching portfolio of the professor but really do not take them seriously. Others profess not to put too much stock in them but take them very seriously. There are many more controversies, such as many students' general suspicion that nothing they say on these forms matters anyway. I clearly overheard the following from two students walking down the hallway the last day of classes after filling out forms: "Did you give a good rating?" "They're all tenured, so what does it matter what I think?" "Yeah, you're right." I butted into the conversation at that point!

In the end, these controversies matter little. The student ratings for each of your courses is part of the permanent record of your performance as a teacher, like it or not. And for the immediate purpose of understanding and improving one's own student ratings, which is the focus of this chapter, the controversy surrounding them is beside the point.

READ AND UNDERSTAND THE FORM

Directing someone to read and understand the form by which they are to be judged in a certain performance may sound like inane advice, but there is more here than can be seen at first glance. Most professors have a vague idea of what the student ratings form requests of the student and the professor. You may read it upon arriving at a new institution but not really read it again reflectively, believing you have a general understanding of the questions. Can you name the eight questions your students are asked on your form, the questions about your teaching and your course? I once counseled a relatively new faculty member who wanted to increase student ratings at the risk of non-contract renewal. This professor could name only one of the five categories within which one must "score" with students on the form. This professor was mildly desperate, obviously intelligent, and had not really read and understood the very instrument that could demolish or promote a career.

There is another more subtle sense of understanding the form at your institution. Often students understand questions in consistently unexpected ways. You should identify how students are understanding certain questions and take this into account when modifying teaching behaviors or modifying courses. For example, one category in the student ratings at my current institution calls for students to rate "active learning" as high level or low level: "How well did the instructor stimulate active learning? (Consider how well the instructor got students actively engaged with the material through writing assignments, critical thinking activities, problem-solving tasks, and whole-class or small group discussions that require student involvement and participation.)" If you had asked me my first year or so at this institution what this question was really asking students to rate, I would have said such things as class discussions and student participation. This was true but too narrow, as a close look at the question and what students actually said showed me. The question lists writing assignments, and I found that my students consistently included the daily one-page reflections they write on that day's readings under the category of active learning. I know this because in the space for comments next to the question, the one-page reflections were often mentioned. The cognitive dissonance was a splash in the face. ("Why are they talking about writing when this question is about discussions?") If I were to modify this course, I would want to take into account how these one-page writings are perceived. Simply deleting or perhaps decreasing them would likely have an effect on "active learning." The point is that professors should not overlook the value of trying to understand the student ratings forms in an open-minded, dynamic, and constructive way.

EACH STUDENT IS A VOTER

At the end of a course, the student you do not care for and the student you would like to clone each have an equal vote about your teaching, a vote aggregated with classmates and delivered to your department chair and dean. It may not be fair, but this is the current situation in which most professors find themselves. At the extremes, you could either completely ignore student ratings or you could pander to students, trying to curry their favor. Neither of these approaches is sensible. Ignoring student ratings is tantamount to saying that students who have participated in and witnessed the course from inception have *no* worthwhile feedback to give on their experience. Equally unreasonable is the approach that compromises the integrity of the course, the professor, and the mission of the institution just to get better "grades" from students.

I advocate treating each student as a voter in the same way that a decent, conscientious politician would. If you ask a local politician to obtain funds for a project, a conscientious politician will not just do it to make you happy. He or she will weigh the request, listen to interest holders, attend to economies of time and money, and so on. In the same way, a professor should treat each student as a voter. This is not pandering to students in order to get their support. If students support you on the student ratings form it is because you have done your job according to the criteria set forth by your institution. Given a

well-designed form, no amount of gratuitous smiling or selective grade infla-
tion is going to change the fact of whether you did your job well or not.
(There are widespread misperceptions that all it takes are these kinds of
activities and other niceties such as knowing student's names or having good
rapport with students.) For example, many student ratings forms have a measure for whether the course was "challenging." Giving someone good grades
when they do not deserve them will not pay off here. My point is that there
is a smart way to deal professionally with students in light of student ratings,
a way that keeps in mind, from the beginning of the term, the last day of class
when students vote for or against the course and the professor.

Consider a local politician who completes a term and is seeking reelec-
tion from his constituents. This politician will present the case for your vote,
and if the case is good, if he has done his job well, you will vote for him. It is
the same in academia, but with a huge caveat. In academia, the judging and
voting is much more subtle. Hopefully a professor does not ever say, "I have
arranged this course brilliantly, so give me a positive evaluation." But it is not
a secret that after the professor has her say on the students' work throughout
the term, the students get to take their one and only shot at being on the
record. And like the political voting booth it is all anonymous.

So from the very first day of the course, and from this peculiar angle of
institutionalized assessment, the professor and the course are being judged in
a way that culminates in student ratings. Throughout a course, students will
share their satisfactions or dissatisfactions with other students in the same
course, almost as if they are trying to recruit voters to their positive or negative opinion about how things are going. How do you present your case to student voters? Indirectly and smartly. First, as the previous section states, you
must read and understand exactly what the institution's form is asking students to judge; what are the criteria? Second, you must treat every interaction (written or oral) with these criteria in mind. Third, you must administer
the student ratings forms in appropriate fashion.

INTERACT WITH STUDENT RATINGS CRITERIA IN MIND

Realistic pedagogical goals, excellent choice of textbooks, sensible course
organization, wonderfully challenging assignments, and good lecturing and
discussions matter in student ratings. And what may matter most to students
is how you interact with them. When you treat every interaction with students keeping the institutions' ratings criteria in mind, you are treating students in the way that your institution values, since they establish the criteria.
Responding to student written work in a prompt, respectful way, personally
addressing students, professionally comparing what they have produced with
the stated assignment criteria, knowing them enough to know how to challenge them, and so on, are subtle ways to present your case to student voters.
This is true for both the D student and the A student. The way in-class ques-

tions or complaints are handled and the way students are attended to in their after-class questions matter at the end. For example, in a large class a particularly shy student has finally decided to seek you out. There may only be one such person-to-person interaction with this particular student who has come up to see you after class on that one day. There are other students queued behind, perhaps the regulars who want you for a moment after class, yet you must recognize how important this moment is for this student. So to be distracted or to look past this student to the others would not be good teaching or smart politics. Recognize this as an important occasion, genuinely attend to this student's questions, and if needed, extend an invitation for the student to visit in office hours or contact you by email.

Other occasions call for equally smart responses, even if the whole interaction is notably unpleasant, as in plagiarism cases. For example, in a plagiarism case that is handled as best as you can, following all the protocols that your institution spells out, the student may be horribly embarrassed or just plain mad at you and at the course. ("Well the workload is too much, so what choice did I have?") How will this student vote at the end of the term? First of all, note that unless you have failed the student or somehow forced him or her to drop the course, the student still gets to vote. Yet a *positive* vote (which is what the institution is seeking from you) is not necessarily lost. A lot depends on how the personal interaction went between you and the student (see chapter 5). Was the interaction about the transgression, or was it about the professor's power? Was the professor antagonistic and demeaning to the student?

As said above, in addition to interaction with students, the whole structure of the course, what materials are used, the workload, the sense and timing of the assignments should all be assumed by the professor to be connected to student ratings. One might object that this is artificial or superficial because the professor is merely bowing down to student power. There is a bowing down here, but it is not to student power; it is to the power of the employer, the institution. Institutions impose the criteria by which the students rate the course and the professor, and professors themselves are often involved on the committees that formulate these criteria. The professor is expected to meet up to these criteria in his or her classroom teaching. Therefore, to keep these criteria forefront, to subtly demonstrate them to students, even if upholding these standards should make a particular student upset, is to do one's job smartly. And I might add, because of the importance of student ratings in one's career, it may be one of the ways at a particular institution to help stabilize or advance one's career.

ADMINISTER STUDENT RATINGS APPROPRIATELY

One model is to administer the student ratings on the last day of the course and make the last day of the course an event that provides some closure to the experience that was this course. Think of it as a sober celebration for students and the professor. It is sweet and sour. The course is virtually accomplished (sweet), and the group will not convene again in this familiar way (sour). The final act of the final course day, other than a final exam or paper, is the student ratings. You must make sure that attendance the last day of class is mandatory and should also save some important content for that day. After the content is finished, and making sure to leave enough time for students to fill out the forms, you should tell the students how you feel about the class and the course. This is not a canned speech and is not a transparent plea for good student ratings, and must be very brief. But it would be crude to pass from the last bit of content immediately to student ratings. This is the last official act of the course as a gathering, and it should be framed and introduced by the professor in a reflective way. It is what a leader does as he or she notes the passing of a remarkable event, in this case, the ending of a course of learning. A professor who has really come to like the students as a class can genuinely tell them so. This is the time. You can acknowledge how much you learned from the students, acknowledge again how their hard work was appreciated, and how you have enjoyed getting to know them. You can also remind the students that just because the course is over, this does not mean academic contact must end and can invite them to seek you out if help is needed in the future.

As will happen with all professors, I remember a class that I really did not like very much. My feeling about the class was neutral at best, as it developed over the term. There were several outstanding students, but the rest seemed to have their minds on something else, even if they did the work. This is not unusual for a required core course consisting of mostly nonmajors. It may have been me, it may have been them, but as any veteran knows, not all groups of students are alike for a professor. I had thought long and hard about what I could say positively and truthfully about the class. The speech between the last of course content and the administration of student ratings was very brief and very different than the speech in another class the same term. To the neutral class I said something like, "I want to take this opportunity to thank you for your work in the course, I have appreciated it very much. If I can be of help to you in the future, please let me know." Then I administered the student ratings. This was a genuine and true statement, as far as it went. Meanwhile, in the class I really liked, my speech started out with "I *really* like this class . . . ," and they knew I meant it. However, in both classes, I did what leaders do when marking a rite of passage or the auspiciousness of an event: I gave a brief address.

Beyond this address, there are three main events in the student ratings ritual. First, there is often some instruction accompanying the forms that needs to be read to the class. If possible, emphasize that students write comments in the space next to the number rating because it is very helpful in improving the course in the future. Second, the forms and pencils are handed out, which can be accomplished by students, and you may ask some student to stay to make sure the completed forms are delivered to the appropriate place. Third, you must leave the room as the forms are filled out. Leave the room and close the door, but stay in the hallway, even if a secondary form is not used (see next section). There are two reasons. First, there may be some question or irregularity (for example, not enough forms), and you should be nearby in this case. Second, it is your chance to say farewell to students as they file out, even if there is a final exam at a later date. Like jury members after their decision, some will not look at you, and others will want to shake your hand. Since liberal arts professors teaching nonmajors are not guaranteed to get "thank you for the course" from students, this is a good opportunity to get a bunch of those.

USE A SECONDARY FORM

Institution-inspired student ratings forms are not the main way to improve your teaching; a secondary form is. Yet by generally improving classroom teaching, a secondary form improves the score on the institution-inspired ratings form. A secondary ratings form is not required by the institution yet administered as if it were. A common example of a secondary ratings form is midterm student ratings. These give the professor some idea of how things are going in the course so that repairs can be made if needed, rather than after the fact. Some professors find these midterm ratings extremely useful. These midterm forms can be the actual form used by the institution or your own secondary form as described next.

A sure-fire way to get the direct response you want is to administer a second special form after the official student ratings forms on the same day of class. You tell students there will be two very short forms and that after they have filled out the first (official) one and put it back into the folder for collection, they will sit back down and wait for the second form. Tell the class to send someone to the hallway to retrieve you after all students have completed the first student ratings form. This secondary student ratings form is a very simple assessment instrument produced by you that gives students a chance to say what went well with the course and professor and what could be improved. With the department name as a heading, and a space for students to fill in the instructor's name, course name, and date, there are only two questions, as if it were an essay exam:

1. Describe one or more things about this instructor and/or course that you found particularly *helpful* and that you would recommend be continued in the future. Please be specific; use examples.

    [*professor leaves a half-page space here*]

2. Describe one or more things about this instructor and/or course that you did *not* find helpful and that you would recommend be changed or dropped. Please be specific; use examples.

Additional questions could be added but should be kept to a minimum. Many professors use secondary forms of various types. This particular secondary form can improve teaching almost immediately, which then improves scores on the primary form.

This form belongs solely to the professor. It gives students real space to expand on the brief comments that the "official" form may or may not have coaxed from them. The professor gets to look at the feedback immediately after grades are turned in. And it gives the professor an easier look at trends. Students tend to write when given a simple question and white space, and the questions are so general they can let go with what they are really thinking. Students who want to list exactly what they found wonderful with the course will list it here. Students who want to vent in some detail have room to do it (and they will). Much of this free-flowing feedback is incredibly helpful. For example, suppose 20 percent of students of their own accord complain about a particular book, responses such as, "The Morris book was irrelevant to what we were studying." This is a strong trend and means the professor needs to attend more closely to how the book is used in the course. Also, since the feedback is almost immediate, this adjustment can happen right away. At many institutions, the next term has already started before the official student ratings forms are returned. However, this secondary instrument can be picked up from the department secretary, still sealed, after grades are turned in. (One could collect and keep them oneself to look at after grades are turned in, but it appears more proper to have the secretary "release" them to you once grades are turned in.)

This immediate feedback on the course also gives you time to prepare for possibly disturbing trends that might appear in the official form. In the case of some disturbing feedback, such as, "The professor let develop a hostile environment for male students," you get to see if this is one student's complaint or several and get to reflect and ruminate on class events to decipher the merits of the complaint. If this complaint does show up in the official student ratings, then the secondary ratings may be pertinent in clearing up what happened, for instance if the chair becomes involved. Also, your own backup measure of how the course went is an unofficial piece of evidence that nonetheless gives a second take on the course. In short, if a couple of students complain about "a hostile environment" in one instrument but not in another, this is significant. Also, if several complained in both, this is significant. Without the second measure, there is no confirmation or disconfirmation, and the second may add more information that helps the professor understand the complaint better.

Mostly, though, the secondary instrument is the best way to get useful feedback on the course. For example, when I first started teaching Introduction to Philosophy, a number of students consistently complained on the secondary instrument that there was "too much Plato" in the course. The comments on the primary student ratings were scattered, but it was easy to see this trend in the secondary instrument. It was not that Plato was too hard; they just wanted more varied philosophy as well. I still do a lot of Plato in introductory courses, but I have adjusted the amount and context, and hence I rarely get this same complaint. The students were right, and it took more than an official form to yield that information. A secondary form exposed the trend in bright lights.

EGO FLUCTUATION, KNOWING THE STANDARD, AND ONLINE RATINGS

There are three other issues worth addressing here: ego fluctuation, knowing the standard, and online ratings. Ego fluctuation is the feeling a professor gets as he or she reads the student comments on sequential student ratings forms: "This course was wonderful, I was riveted to philosophy, what a surprise," and on the next piece of paper, "Boring, boring, boring." These are (partial) actual comments from my secondary instrument by various students in *one* course, neither of which by themselves is very helpful, unless the latter was a trend. But with the secondary form, students tend to elaborate on the positive and the negative, so these exclamations are just the lead. Still, with this kind of fluctuation in student preferences, it would be an error for a professor to believe his or her own press. There are bound to be terminally disengaged students, as well as upset students in each course: upset because they had to take a required course outside their major, upset because you ruined their GPA, upset because they were busted for plagiarism in the course, and so on. But if around 20 percent of a class found the course boring, for example, that is a trend that needs to be addressed. The actual experience of reading the student comments, especially when using a secondary instrument that encourages open, lengthy comments, can be joyful one moment and painful the next. The point here is that the best practice is to look for trends and dismiss the high and low votes, as judges do in some gymnastic competitions. If they are all high votes, that is fantastic. If there are many low votes, work needs to be done. Listen to what they are saying when they expand past their exclamations, looking for trends, even if it is difficult to keep an even keel.

Know what the standard score on student ratings is at your institution. Most institutions have an average for the school or for a department. Find out what it is. Your chair and dean know what is expected. You may far exceed the average, even if others are tenured or tenure-track, and you are not. However, you may think you are doing fine on this institutional measure, yet you fall short of average. Asking fellow professors what their scores are is dicey. Unless you see them in writing ("show me"), then you will never know how inflated the score is. A professor's student ratings are usually a closely held secret, but a chair or dean knows the aggregate and can tell you where you should be. Also, annual review forms that apply to tenured and tenure-track professors often have a breakdown of where scores should be, for example, for merit pay. A chair, dean, friendly colleague, or departmental secretary should be able to provide the form, if you are not tenured or tenure-track.

Students can now publicly rate their professors online, and they do. For example, put in a professor's name and institution at a Web site such as rate-myprofessors.com, and up pops student ratings with comments. These ratings are fraught with even more bias than the standard ratings forms used by the institution and can ask for patently irrelevant information such as if the professor is "hot." However, this does not mean these sites should be dismissed out of hand. Every professor should check what is being said on the World-Wide Web by current or former students. First, it is another measure, and you may learn something from the comments. Second, assume your current students have looked you up before registering for your course. If so, you need to be aware of what is being said about you in public, in case it drives certain questions or concerns in class or in private conversations with students. Third, look up colleagues. There are professors in your department or school who are known to be great teachers. What do students say about them? What can you learn from what they say? Though flawed, this is as close as you will get to reading their private student ratings.

Understanding student ratings is a way to improve them, and improving student ratings or maintaining excellent scores is one way to show your institution that you are competent at your job and that you value what they value in good teaching.

CHAPTER EIGHT

Conclusion

————— ◆ ———

No one controls exactly how learning occurs in the classroom. The professor designs the opportunities, like the gardener prepares the soil. Neither nurturer precisely controls the growth. In fact, what appears to be a sucker growth may be a splendid new branch.

As a graduate student assisting a noted and popular professor, I recall the day that the classroom erupted in rapid-fire questioning about the nature of "freedom." The professor did his best to take on the snowballing questions as they came from every corner of the large classroom. His responses were hesitant and thoughtful, and he looked a bit uncomfortable. These second-year nonmajors were making him dance intellectually and politely refused to stop playing the music. It was an unprecedented class day, late in a solidly taught but otherwise uneventful course.

The professor was exasperated after the class session. As we walked together, almost muttering he said, "That was a disaster. It was the worst class I've had in a long time." I disagreed. I told him the class session was extraordinary, better than any I had witnessed in my semesters assisting him. The students were alive with genuine concern for the question of freedom, challenging the professor to dig deep to respond to their concern, not taking incomplete or flawed responses as truth—exactly how he would have wanted them to be if he could have planned it. He could not anticipate this spontaneous and wonderful hour of classroom teaching and learning, he could not control the students' learning, and he could not control his feelings of vulnerability and inadequacy. Since he was deeply wrapped in the event as the main participant, he could not immediately recognize this event as positive. Amidst all the uncertainties and anxieties on the part of the teacher and students, that moment was a memorable classroom learning event, and what matters is that it happened because of consistently inspired lecturing, smart arrangement of materials and assignments, and a superb classroom atmosphere. In the classroom, we have good days, mediocre days, and bad days. Sometimes what we perceive as our worst days are students' best days, as this "freedom" story illustrates. But this story also illustrates that excellent practices are more likely to yield excellent results, even if those results are beyond our control and expectations, and even if what is actually a splendid new branch appears to us as sucker growth.

College teaching is the strangest of jobs. At the end of a class session, we may not know how it went, or we may think we know exactly how it went. Yet there remains the possibility to wildly misdiagnose the brainwave and heartbeat of that day's class. This untidiness or openness in the learning and teaching process is necessary. We must realize that for liberal arts and sciences disciplines, uncertainty is built into a superb class session. At some level, our goal with nonmajors is to encourage their interest in our discipline and to see how it relates to their daily lives, their futures, and the discipline they have chosen for their majors. In order to achieve this goal we must strive to lead them to question all these things by the end of a class session, to question their daily lives, their futures, their discipline. In short, a class session that tightly sews up the holey cloak of learning is a failure. Students need to walk out of each liberal arts and sciences class session with a horizon of unease, ambivalence, ambiguity, and vagueness and with the intellectual tools and cognitive lenses of that course's discipline to start to connect that horizon to the ground upon which they walk.

Better classroom teaching to nonmajors brings about better questioning. If we are doing our jobs, students question better about our discipline, for example about its worth. They question about the discipline of their own major courses in comparison to what they are learning in our course. They question because they care, they have become engaged. As we prepare for each class day, devising how to deliver to our students the certainties of fact, principle, process, and theory, we must ask ourselves loudly: "How will I create a clearing in the student's world for the appearance of active uncertainty?" This active uncertainty—the presence of a challenging horizon of doubt—gives birth to inquiry and specifically to the genuine desire to know more about a given discipline, even if it is not that student's major.

Index